M000309710

The
Freelance Writer's
Handbook

By Dennis E. Hensley
> *Writing for Profit*
> *The Freelancer* (with Stanley Field)
> *Positive Workaholism*
> *Uncommon Sense*
> *Staying Ahead of Time*

By Holly G. Miller
> *First Person Singular* (with Jerry Jones)
> *The Power Lift* (with Bill Ashpaugh)

By Dennis E. Hensley and Holly G. Miller
(pen name Leslie Holden)
> *The Legacy of Lillian Parker*
> *The Compton Connection*
> *The Caribbean Conspiracy*

The
Freelance Writer's
Handbook

How to Succeed in a Competitive Business

Dennis E. Hensley
Holly G. Miller

Harper & Row, Publishers, New York
Cambridge, Philadelphia, San Francisco, Washington
London, Mexico City, São Paulo, Singapore, Sydney

THE FREELANCE WRITER'S HANDBOOK. Copyright © 1987 by Dennis E. Hensley and Holly G. Miller. All rights reserved. Printed in the United States of America. No part of this book may be used or reproduced in any manner whatsoever without written permission except in the case of brief quotations embodied in critical articles and reviews. For information address Harper & Row, Publishers, Inc., 10 East 53rd Street, New York, N.Y. 10022. Published simultaneously in Canada by Fitzhenry & Whiteside Limited, Toronto.

FIRST EDITION

Designed by Abigail Sturges
Copyeditor: Dorian Hastings
Index by Maro Riofrancos

Library of Congress Cataloging-in-Publication Data

Hensley, Dennis E., 1948–
    The freelance writer's handbook.

    Includes index.
    1. Authorship. I. Miller, Holly, II. Title.
PN153.H43   1987   808'.02   87-45055
ISBN 0-06-055096-1   87 88 89 90 91 MPC 10 9 8 7 6 5 4 3 2 1
ISBN 0-06-096203-8 (pbk.)   87 88 89 90 91 MPC 10 9 8 7 6 5 4 3 2 1

Contents

This book is dedicated to Rose Hensley and Phil Miller, in recognition of their continuous support and encouragement of all our writing efforts

Foreword

Lessons from the Professionals

The Saturday Evening Post has a long tradition of boosting the careers of talented authors just breaking into print—writers like Jack London, Kurt Vonnegut, Mary Roberts Rinehart, Paul Gallico, and William Saroyan—and it's a tradition we want to continue.

One of the pluses of my job as associate publisher of the *Post* is traveling the country and meeting new writers. Article ideas often are shared shyly at first; then, when the authors realize they have a sympathetic listener, they become more enthusiastic, more animated. I get caught up in the ideas and the enthusiasm, too. Send us a query, I'll say. Or, if it's a time-dated topic, I'll invite them to submit entire manuscripts.

Unfortunately, the correspondence that results often doesn't live up to the idea that prompted it. The excitement the author exhibited toward his topic in spoken terms doesn't translate onto the written page. The color is gone; the sense of freshness is absent. Where are the lively quotes? The on-target description? The insightful background info? Frequently, the idea has grown to such proportions that it can't be covered in depth in 3,000 words. In an effort to write something *important*, the novice author has forfeited focus. On more than one occasion I've been reminded of E. B. White's advice: "Don't write about *Man*," he said, "write about *a* man."

Whenever these superficial glossings arrive "over the transom," time doesn't permit a critique by our editorial staff; they're too immersed in the nitty-gritty details of producing a magazine. What irony—we editors are too busy to develop and train new writers, yet if we had sufficient writers who were developed and trained, we'd have more time. *If only there were a way to introduce a couple of seasoned professionals for some serious shoptalk with these enthusiastic beginners,* I've often thought.

Well, this book promises to do just that. Dennis Hensley and Holly Miller have jointly shared bylines on a series of books and have earned credits individually from such publications as *Reader's Digest, Writer's Digest, TV Guide, The Writer, People, The Christian Writer* (now *Writer's Inspirational Newsletter*), and *Online Today*. Drawing on these experiences, they've put together ten chapters that trace the writing process from idea to interview to invoice. Not only do they share tips on how to produce more memorable copy, but also how to sell it several times over to uncommon markets.

Writers today wear many hats . . . those of the creative "genius" (idea person), sleuth (researcher), author, editor, salesman, and publicist. They have to have sensitive souls and tough skins, be aggressive listeners and placid agitators. If they aren't writing, they are at least reading someone else's writing. They love words, delight in expanding their vocabulary, yet communicate in easy-to-understand terms.

If all this sounds like a tall order, it is. How do you go about filling it? The first step may be as simple as picking up this book. And the second is turning the page. . . .

—Robert L. Silvers
Associate Publisher
The Saturday Evening Post

Acknowledgments

We wish to acknowledge certain mentors, friends, and business associates who have done much to advance our writing careers to a point that made this book possible, most notably: Neil Ringle, John Brady, Bill Brohaugh, Tom Noton, Steve Summers, Rita Winters, Sally Stuart, Jody Molnar, Clayton Carlson, Lou and Jonellen Heckler, Phil Johnson, Janet Hoover Thoma, John R. Ingrisano, Dr. Frances Rippy, Marilyn Bailey, Jean Brannon, Rose A. Adkins, Tom Clark, Dr. Tom Koontz, Dr. Earl Conn, Ted Kreiter, Nancye Hawes, and Patrick McKeand.

1

How to Be a
Competitive Writer

All writers worry about competition. And I probably more than most.

In 1984, word was out that the Thomas Nelson Company was going to hire some lucky author to write a book about the forty-year history of Youth for Christ International. This project carried with it a substantial author expense account, a large advance against royalties, and an all-expense-paid research trip to Asia.

I wanted that contract.

But so did five other qualified writers. And we all were politicking like crazy to win editorial committee votes.

Finally, a phone call came to me.

"Good news for you," the trade books editor told me. "Our first choice for the project is now no longer available. The contract can be offered to you if you're still interested."

"Thanks," I said, swallowing hard, ". . . I think."

Somehow, winning the contract by default took a lot of the joy out of the victory.

It reminded me of the time, years earlier, when I had asked Tex Ritter during an interview how he had been chosen to sing the title song for the movie *High Noon*. Tex had winced at my question and answered, "Frankie Laine had laryngitis that week."

Apparently, competition abounds in every line of work.

THE COMPETITIVE EDGE

Now, don't misunderstand me: I took the Nelson contract (and the cash advance and the free ten-day research trip to Hong Kong,

Japan, and Macao) and I was genuinely grateful to the Nelson people for their confidence in me. And I feel that I eventually wrote a good book for them, too. (I must have, because they have since offered me numerous other contracts.) But the point is this: Situations like that constantly remind me that writers *are* in competition.

I once heard Clayton Carlson, West Coast vice-president of Harper & Row, put this matter into perspective in an address he gave before the Willamette Writers' Conference in Oregon.

Said Carlson, "There are two kinds of writers, and both are needed by editors and readers. One is the artist, the writer who can devote six or eight years to developing a novel which will endure for decades. The other is the competitive writer, the person who gives his all to be the first to report on the fire downtown or to develop a column with a new slant or to write a trendy book which will appeal to the immediate needs of the masses. Of these two types of writers, I don't know which has the greater challenge or the harder struggle."

I long ago settled for myself which kind of writer I am. I don't have the talent to be an artist, but I do have the guts and savvy to be a competitive writer. I play to win, and usually do.

ONE FOR THE MONEY . . .

In 1975, I moved from Michigan to Muncie, Indiana. My wife and I bought our first home, started our family, and I began working at Ball State University on my doctor's degree in English. As a Vietnam veteran I received $3,175 per year schooling allowance on the G.I. Bill and I earned an additional $3,300 by teaching freshman composition part time at the college.

Now, I don't know if you've ever tried to make house and car payments, pay utility bills, and feed and clothe three people, as well as pay for tuition and books, on just $6,475 per year, but I'm here to tell you that it can't be done.

I desperately needed more money. However, I discovered that no one wanted to hire a person who couldn't work on a set schedule.

Finally, though, I did find someone. I got lucky. Sort of.

The arts and features editor of the local newspaper worked out a deal with me: I would be able to come to work whenever I had time. The editor would keep a list of article ideas handy. Whenever I came in, if anything was available he would give me an assignment. I'd go cover it and write it up and turn it in, and then he would credit me with fifteen dollars toward my next pay voucher. Every two weeks he would tally the number of fifteen-dollar features I had written, and he would have the accounting department cut me a check for that total. It wasn't high finance, but it was a job. So I took it.

My work was strictly freelance. I qualified for no set salary, no vacation pay, no medical plan, no retirement benefits. And, with the inspiration of desperation, I learned to be very competitive. I grabbed as many "open" assignments as were available. I'd come in at 7 a.m. on Saturdays and work on general feature stories until 6 p.m., then grab a snack and make it just in time for the opening curtain of the 7 p.m. presentation of the community theater (or a local concert). When the presentation ended at 10 p.m., I'd hightail it back to the newsroom and write a review for Sunday morning's edition. I'd never get home before midnight.

On weekdays, I'd pick up assignments on the way to the campus and work on them between classes and at lunchtime. I'd use the telephone to get local quotes, I'd pump the profs for professional commentary, and I'd use the campus library to verify statistical research. On my way home in the evening, I'd stop by the newsroom, find an empty desk and an unused typewriter, then pound out whatever I'd worked on that day. After turning it in, I would go home, have dinner, and then work on either the record review column I wrote for Saturday's paper or the book review column I wrote for the Sunday arts page.

Whenever I was at the newspaper, I took a lot of kidding about being "standoffish." If the staff would go down to the press room or into the circulation department to share some cake and coffee to celebrate someone's promotion or retirement or new baby, I wouldn't join them. I'd sit and type. If the telephone rang, I wouldn't answer it; I'd just go on typing. If strangers came into the newsroom to deliver press releases or to ask to speak to a reporter, I'd always direct them to someone else (someone on salary) and I'd go on typing.

My colleagues at the newspaper knew the pressure I was under from my doctoral studies and my financial strains. They teased but tolerated me. At first, at least.

But one day, the paper's managing editor came by my desk and nodded at me. "You know, Hensley," he said, "if I had three more like you, I could cut this news staff in half."

I waited for him to chuckle, but he never did. He was serious. And it was right after that incident that the salaried reporters began to show up earlier for work, stay later, and work harder.

Did that make me happy?—give me a sense of accomplishment?—make me feel proud of the influence I had had on that newsroom?

Actually, no. In truth, that was the last thing in the world that I wanted to have happen to those reporters. Why? Because once the other reporters started scrambling for open assignments and began to log extra hours and fight for bylines and column inches, it meant I had to start working all that much harder in order to maintain my level of earnings.

Competition had had its rewards. But it also had had its costs.

I learned early that there was no resting on laurels in the field of writing. In fact, there was no resting on *anything*. It was all hustle, hustle, hustle.

And I'm so glad I learned that fact *early*. Knowing it has shaped my whole career.

AHHH-SO!

Competitive writing and judo have a lot in common. To become good at either, one must have a thorough understanding of leverage.

Let's face facts: If we set aside Mailer, Michener, Tom Wolfe, Stephen King, and a handful of others, most of us freelancers are fairly equal in talent. We've learned about the five Ws and the H (who, what, when, where, why, and how), we've mastered typing, and we've all had some sort of educational or field experiences. So what's going to make any one of us any more successful than the next person if writing talent alone won't do it? Leverage, that's what.

In this business, you need symbolic levers and winches and pulleys and fulcrums the same way you do in corporate management or military hierarchies. It's not how much you weigh that counts, but how you maneuver that weight. Let's take a minute to look at the rules of the leveraging game.

Rule 1: *Always Work to Expand Your Professional Contacts.*
You can't hitch your wagon to just one horse if you plan to make it across the desert.

In the Old Testament, Joseph won Pharaoh's approval and served him well for many years. But the minute a new king assumed power, Joseph was unemployed (Exodus 1:8). That lesson is pertinent to writers. No matter how "buddy-buddy" you may be with one key editor at a publishing house (or magazine or newspaper), you'd better not rest your entire career on that relationship. If that editor resigns, transfers, retires, or dies, you'll suddenly find yourself at square one.

I currently serve as a contributing editor for six national magazines. My twelve books have been published by four different publishing houses. With a range of contacts that diverse, I don't lose sleep over job security. My old journalism professor once told me, "There's something to be said for loyalty, Hensley, and that something is vulnerability."

He was right.

You should take every opportunity available to expand your contacts. Begin by attending writers' conferences and putting your manuscripts directly into the hands of visiting editors and publishers. Invite them to coffee or lunch. Put your face in front of them; smile; pass out your business cards; send follow-up "reminder" letters of your meetings. Hustle.

Next, lean on your writer friends to make some introductions for you. Have them take you along sometime to an author–editor luncheon confab; have them recommend you for any assignments they are offered but are unable to take on. Also, ask around and find an already-published author who needs a co-author on a new project. (Entering a publishing house through the back door still gets you inside.)

Constantly force yourself to learn about new markets. Read trade and technical magazines, especially. Send for their guidelines for writers and learn how to crack some of the specialty markets. (For more information on this, see Chapter 8 of this book.) Competition is less intense here and you can rise to the top quicker. I am neither an optometrist nor an optician, yet I am currently a columnist and contributing editor for *Insight* magazine. I am not a cosmetologist, yet I'm a contributing editor for *ShopTalk*. I studied these trade journals, learned all about their markets, and proved I could write for them. You can do likewise.

Rule 2: *Be Aggressive at Multiple Marketing.*
People are amazed when they read that I have had more than fifteen hundred bylines in magazines and newspapers. They often ask, "How did you ever find time to write fifteen hundred articles?" I answer, "I didn't. During the past twenty years I've written about eight hundred and fifty articles, but I've sold many of them from three to ten different times."

I call this hyper-multiple-marketing. All competitive writers are engaged in it.

You cannot sell all rights to your articles and be competitive. It's impossible. If you work two weeks doing interviews and research for a major feature, and then one week writing it, and a fourth week revising, typing, and submitting it, you'll produce only a dozen features a year.

And that's O.K., as long as you sell this year's dozen again next year to new markets while you are writing a dozen new features. At the end of five years you'll have sixty features in the mail simultaneously, and believe me, that's being competitive. But if you sell all rights, you will be starting from scratch with each new assignment. You'll have one manuscript in the mail at a time, and hyper-multiple-marketers like myself (and there are plenty of us) will just out-leverage you and completely crowd you out of the marketplace.

Competitive writers only write about topics they feel they can modify for a variety of audiences. (In 1975, I wrote a piece called, "How to Be an Effective Listener," which has sold to a total of twenty-one markets and earned me more than $6,500.)

Competitive writers retain copyright ownership of their articles and only sell "all rights" when a publisher pays a rate equivalent to what the author would earn if he or she had made three or four sales of that article.

Consider this: The owner of a champion race horse does not give his horse to the racetrack's owner just because the horse won a race there. No, no. The horse's owner accepts the purse money and then moves the horse to another track so that the horse can win there, too. Speaking metaphorically, if you give away ownership of your manuscript just because the manuscript won its first race, you are scratching yourself from all future races. You are eliminating yourself from competition. That's not very smart on your part. Later in this book we will go into more detail about multiple marketing, cyclical marketing, and series marketing.

Rule 3: *Diversify Your Talents.*
Simple logic will tell you that the more diversified you are in your writing, the more reasons an editor will have to call you for a variety of assignments. Somehow, writers are usually blind to this, however.

A woman told me recently that she had been attending the same writers' conference faithfully for six years, yet she still was earning only 5 cents per word for her manuscripts. "I now have six years of experience, but I'm earning the same money I was earning when I began," she complained. "Why is that? My friends are earning much more."

Upon questioning the woman further, I discovered that each year that she had attended the conference she had taken the week-long course in poetry. She had studied no other topics.

"And there's your problem, madam," I explained. "You really don't have six years of experience; you have one year of experience that you have repeated five more times. You've never expanded your skills. The other writers in your car pool these past six years have moved on to courses in photography, short story and novel writing, interviewing skills, and humor writing. They're earning more now because they have more markets to compete in."

How about you? Have you been putting blinders on your eyes?

If you have been ignoring romance writing or children's literature or sports reporting or playwriting because these literary expressions didn't appeal to you, you have eliminated yourself from competing in some very lucrative markets. Instead of being competitive, you've crossed yourself off the playing card. The next time you attend a writers' conference, purposely register for a class that makes you feel out of your league. You'll be surprised at what you'll learn.

Rule 4: *Seek High Visibility.*

Have you ever asked yourself why Stephen King and Robert Ludlum do commercials for a credit card company . . . or why George Plimpton fronts for a video game company . . . or why Mickey Spillane appears in beer commercials on TV? No doubt they get big bucks for those sorts of things, but I've got to be thinking that none of those writers is running short on steaks and caviar these days. So why bother?

Frankly, it gives them visibility. All writers can benefit from visibility.

If you walk into a bookstore and you see a book with a bland title like *Carrie,* you'll probably pass right by it. But if the book says, "Stephen King's *Carrie,*" and you think, "Hey, that's the weirdo who does that ghoulish commercial on TV," you'll probably stop and pick up the book and read the dust jacket. This leads to a sale. Hence, the more visibility an author gains, the more competitive he or she becomes in holding a share of the market.

Last year I was a guest instructor at thirty-one writers' conferences and workshops across the country. In seventeen of the places I visited, I made arrangements in advance to appear on local radio and TV talk shows. After five such interviews, the questions became very repetitive. But I acted each time as though each question were a fresh idea. It was worth the effort. The visibility helped sell a lot of my books.

If you've published a book, you should write and call your area media outlets and make yourself available for interviews. You should also work with your publishers to line up phone interviews between yourself and out-of-state reviewers and interviewers. Furthermore, you should visit bookstores to help organize your own autograph parties. Keep in mind: Silence is not golden, it's just plain yellow.

Whenever articles are published about you, have hundreds of copies duplicated to use as handout promo pieces at writers' clubs, conferences, and booksellers' conventions.

Argue with your publisher to get your photograph on the dust jackets of your books. Be visible any way you can be. It'll give you a competitive edge over the "invisible" writers.

Rule 5: *Be a Wheeler-Dealer.*
Competitive writers are not afraid to push their luck. The average writer is usually overjoyed if he learns that a publisher has accepted his book proposal, but the competitive writer will usually ask, "Can we just go ahead and expand this contract to cover all three books I plan to do on this topic?" It sounds pushy, and it is, but it's worth it.

In 1980, I was asked to write a book on time management for the Bobbs-Merrill/R & R Newkirk Publishing Company. I did write it; but not before we made some major changes in the original "standard" contract. When my book *Staying Ahead of Time* was released in 1981, it was serialized in R & R Newkirk's *Sales Builder* magazine, copies were made part of the company's "Financial Planning" marketing kit, and I was hired as the keynote speaker for the company's annual sales conference.

To be truly competitive, you must compete for cash returns in all direct *and* tangent markets related to your areas of writing expertise. It all comes back to what I told you I learned long ago: You've got to hustle, hustle, hustle.

SUMMARY

Erma Bombeck once wrote a column about a man she met who *wasn't* writing a book. She'd never before met anyone who wasn't either writing a book or planning to write a book. Said Erma to the man, "When did you first get this idea not to write a book?"

The Bombeck parody is hilarious, but it points out that writers (and would-be writers) are everywhere. To compete against them, you've got to know how to use leverage. That is the whole purpose of this book: to teach you the writing and marketing skills needed to provide you with a competitive edge. So, read and study each chapter and work on the Action Items.

Become competitive!

Action Items

1. Determine what kind of writer you want to be. Do you have the patience, creativity, and training to become an artist who writes novels? Do you have the energy, mental agility, and street sense it takes to be a competitive writer? Make a list of your writing preferences, your areas of training in writing, and your writing goals. See what you can discover about yourself.

2. Staying current with new markets is part of what it takes to be a competitive writer. Make a trip to your local newsstand and buy copies of the writing trade publications such as *The Writer, Writer's Inspirational Journal, Writer's Digest, Writer's Yearbook, Folio,* and *Writer's Journal.* Become familiar with the markets each of these periodicals focuses upon. Consider subscribing to one or more of them.

3. Spend a couple of hours browsing in the periodicals room of your local library. Scan the tables of contents of a variety of publications. How many of those articles are on topics you could have just as easily written about? Which important topics are *not* being reported on? Make a list. This will be your starting point for an "ideas file."

Suggested Additional Readings

The Freelancer: A Writer's Guide to Success by Dennis E. Hensley and Stanley Field (Indianapolis: Poetica Press, 1984).

Getting Your Foot in the Editorial Door by Thomas A. Noton (Lakeland, Fla.: TCW Group, 1984).

The Writer's Craft edited by John Hersey (New York: Knopf, Inc., 1974).

2

Knowing What Impresses an Editor

Somewhere out there in the world of overworked Selectrics, chalky patches of Ko-rec-type, and dog-eared SASEs (self-addressed, stamped envelopes for return replies), lurks a freelance writer with a can of gold spray paint.

Her name? I don't remember; neither do I recall her manuscript. But who could forget the 14-karat manila envelopes with the Midas touch that arrived periodically at the editorial offices of *The Saturday Evening Post?* The writer's strategy was simple: Spray one 9 × 12-inch envelope with an eye-catching metallic mist and wait for the magazine's slush editor (sorry, but *slush* is slang for *unsolicited manuscripts*) to gravitate to the glowing submission.

The plan backfired, of course, when said editor lifted said manuscript from said slush and found himself immediately dubbed "Goldfinger" by his scoffing colleagues.

'Nuff said.

Another ingenious freelancer, this one with a long history of rejection slips, once set out to soothe his wounded pride by indulging in a game of stump the staff. Convinced his manuscripts were never *really* read by an editor, he decided to prove his theory by gluing together every third and fourth page of his submission. That way, when the article was returned—and they always were—he would know his submission had never been considered because the pages would still be firmly fastened.

Imagine the frustration of the magazine editor struggling to evaluate an article she had to steam apart. Ouch. No sale. I know, because I was that editor.

One last anecdote: A fiction writer from Denver used to periodically send me ho-hum stories that were topped off with cover letters composed entirely of words and phrases snipped from newspapers and magazines. They were like ransom notes, but I'm proud to say I never succumbed to the demands. I only wished the author had spent more of her time and creativity on writing and less on cutting and pasting.

Gimmicks don't sell manuscripts. In the competitive world of magazine publishing, the buck stops with the editor, and so does your manuscript. Forget the cryptic cover letter; more than spray paint is required if a word-weary editor is to notice your writing, and more than a glue stick is needed to make him hold on to it. I've sat on both sides of the editor's desk, as buyer and seller, and can attest that from either vantage point the message is the same: Only *professionalism* moves manuscripts, and only the writer who exhibits, *exudes*, professionalism is going to move editors.

So how do you acquire this professionalism? With practice. Lots of practice. And it all begins with the query letter, since this is your first contact with a publication's editorial staff. An editor is more likely to be impressed by the writer who sends a query rather than one who sends a complete manuscript. Why? Because the query cuts down on valuable time—yours and his. A one-page, single-spaced letter may take five minutes to read and evaluate, but a complete article may require an hour. If the idea you propose in your query sparks interest, the editor may offer suggestions: "No more than a thousand words, please"; "Could you change the slant to include more background?"; "Incorporate a few more quotes from the third expert. . . ." If you've already completed your manuscript, you're back at square one because the rules of the game have been changed.

Not only does a query letter take less time to prepare than a manuscript, it also returns a verdict—good or bad—faster. Whereas a manuscript must work its way up through a hierarchy of readers before it is scrutinized by an editor, the query goes directly to someone in the upper half of the masthead. (A magazine's masthead is merely the listing, somewhere near the table of contents, of key editorial personnel.)

Finally, a query makes sense because it saves cents. Postage is a major line item in every freelancer's budget, and a query letter, folded in thirds and inserted in a business-size envelope, is going to cost far less than a multipage manuscript mailed flat in a plain brown wrapper.

PLAYING THE MARKET

Long before you sit down and actually compose your query, you've got to decide where you're going to send it. Here, you'll do well to heed the advice of Professor Harold Hill because, "Ya gotta know the territory." There's no such thing as a generic query, equally at home in the editorial offices of *Good Housekeeping, Guideposts, Atlantic Monthly,* or the *National Enquirer.* Magazines, like people, have personalities. Even a publication that falls loosely under the umbrella title of women's or men's or sports or computer magazine may differ greatly from others in the same category. *Cosmo, Savvy,* and *Today's Christian Woman* are all magazines geared to females, but each reaches out to different women within the general audience labeled "women." So, indulge in a little market research. Don't waste an editor's time by sending him a proposal totally inappropriate for his publication. Remember, magazine writing is among the few professions where the practitioner can sit with feet propped, sipping Coke Classic, scanning a copy of *McCall's,* and claim to be working. But that's what it takes. A writer must be thoroughly versed in her markets and should spend part of every day tracking them. If a publication isn't available on the newsstand or at the library, sample copies can be secured from editorial headquarters for the price of an issue and a SASE. And while you're corresponding, why not ask for the publication's guidelines? These are free and include data on what the magazine buys, its pay scale, photo needs, length requirements, and deadlines. File the information with the sample issues for future reference.

Even after you've identified the likely destination for your query, you're not done with your homework yet. Have you decided which staff editor should be on the receiving end of the correspondence? Impress him by knowing not only his name, but also his title. None of this "Dear Editor" stuff. Suggestion: Send your query to either a senior editor, articles editor, or assistant managing editor. They're the roll-up-your-sleeves types who are immersed in getting an issue out the door and into subscribers' hands.

Remember that the curse of every magazine staffer is a set of X-ray eyes that even Superman would envy. These are eyes that, like it or not, catch every typo, stall at each misspelling and couldn't leap over a grammatical mistake with a single bound if they wanted to. *Be careful.* Don't turn an editor off before you turn him on. Your query must be flawlessly typed, meticulously crafted, single-spaced, and brief. After writing it, set it aside for a day or two before giving it a final reading, slipping in the SASE, and sending it on its way. You may find an error or two yourself.

So much for the mechanics. What about content? What can you possibly say in a query that will cause an editor to pause midyawn and respond, Yes! he'd like to read the whole manuscript?

It takes a super idea; an idea only *you* can supply. And sometimes these gems surface in unlikely places. Like in Muncie, Indiana.

I once had the opportunity to interview *Hee Haw* star Lulu Roman when she was passing through Muncie, booked for an afternoon gospel concert. I had no market in mind for the story and honestly wondered if I'd have any luck selling it. Lulu was an interesting personality, all right, but hardly a household name unless you were a fan of cornpone humor delivered via Saturday night syndication.

Still, writers have to take chances, so early one Sunday morning I sleepily drove thirty miles east to keep my date with Lulu. When I met her agent at the motel I began quizzing him for a news angle. I asked if she was involved in any new projects. Not really, he said. Was there anything she truly liked to talk about? I questioned, fishing. Nothing in particular, he replied, not biting. Anything she didn't like to discuss—like her weight? He brightened and explained that Lulu was on a diet and already had lost fifty pounds. It was my turn to brighten. Here was a woman who had built a career on being fat and she was now determined to trim her girth in half! Maybe I had a story after all.

The interview went well; Lulu was witty, candid, and full of quotable anecdotes. As I drove home that night I tried to sort out our visit and determine where my query would most likely fire some interest. *Think big*, I decided, as I chose *TV Guide*. After all, Lulu was best known in that medium; and besides, I had heard the magazine paid well. Extremely well.

When I sat down at my typewriter the next day, I knew my greatest obstacle would be convincing the editor that I, an unknown writer from the provinces, could deliver a publishable article. I labored for two days over the letter before finally coming up with this version, addressed to Mr. Andrew Mills, assistant managing editor, whose name I plucked from the masthead of an issue I borrowed from a friend.

Dear Mr. Mills:

Three months ago Lulu Roman lumbered onto the bathroom scales to receive some bad news: 318 pounds of it. Her knees buckled in painful protest. Burrowing in hay mounds, popping out of cornfields and bellying up to the bar at the Hee Haw truck stop were becoming increasingly difficult. The solution was as plain as the chins on her face—a carefully supervised diet, heavy on the cottage cheese and sans all things chocolate.

"I've spent 34 years of my life being a fatty and I want to spend the next 34 being skinny," says Lulu, now an agile 268 pounds and fading. Since her role on *Hee Haw* was built around her round, firm, and fully-packed physique, she sought the blessing of the show's producer before embarking on the high protein and rabbit food routine. He applauded her goal— a size-10 dress—and promised to add the pads as she subtracted the pounds.

I recently spent an afternoon with Lulu discussing her famous figure, why it grew to such renowned proportions, and what prompted her to change all this. We talked about *Hee Haw*, her battle with drugs, her years in an orphanage, and her born-again career as a gospel singer.

With your permission I'd like to send you on speculation an article introducing viewers to the new Lulu. The story is timely because fans will be seeing less of Lulu—literally— when the newly taped segments are aired in January.

My qualifications? I'm a former senior editor of *The Saturday Evening Post* and currently manage a midsized daily newspaper.

Sincerely,

Holly Miller

Happily, Andrew Mills liked the idea. More important, he liked the way I presented it. My query had to sell Lulu Roman as a subject *and* Holly Miller as a writer. The editor needed to be teased by the topic and entertained by the style. The last paragraph of the query, the one dealing with qualifications, really wasn't necessary. By the time the editor reached that point, he knew if the proposal was right for him.

Postscript: Yes, the article sold . . . twice! After it was published in the domestic *TV Guide,* it was picked up by the Canadian version. As I cashed two—not one but two—checks for the same story, I remember thinking that Dennis Hensley would be proud of me.

AIM TO PLEASE

Impress an editor by inviting his or her input. In your query, ask for directions. And when he offers advice, follow it to the letter. If he says he could use 2,000 words, don't mount your soapbox and turn in 6,000. If he says he wants to see it by December 1, don't send it in March with an apology that you were "just too busy."

Help the editor by suggesting where suitable illustrations—sharp black-and-white glossy prints or 35 mm color slides—might be located. If you take pictures youself, include one in your query as a sample of the work you can do. If you have a local photographer with whom you like to work, mention his name. Unless you're dealing with a very large magazine, the editor will be grateful for your help. In fact, it may land you the sale. Getting top-rate photos is a big problem for smaller publications that don't have the luxury of a photo staff.

As the editor comes to appreciate your talents, let him know you appreciate his burdens. Magazine deadlines *are* etched in stone and are not subject to change. Production schedules are prepared a year in advance, and if all editorial material for the December issue is due September 30, the editor is responsible for keeping the date. Any delay costs money. Earn an editor's trust by being on time. If you do, he'll remember you when he schedules a last-minute interview with Julio Iglesias and needs a writer to jet down to Nassau in a hurry. (Julio was a dear; details in Chapter 5.)

On the topic of deadlines, be aware that most magazines work with a three-to-six-month lead time. August is the month to write the New Year's resolution story, and November is when you should be putting Memorial Day features on paper. Many a magazine editor searches the slush for Christmas fiction in July but comes up with little more than light summer romance. Most writers can't seem to get in the mood for Christmas until they have chestnuts roasting on an open fire. Well, fire up the chestnuts in July, because by winter they're out of season.

LITTLE THINGS MEAN A LOT

If your query letter is a success and an editor says, yes, he'd like to see the full manuscript, don't waste time. You've tested the water with your toe, now you've got your whole foot in the pond, but you're not stroking for gold yet. Your final draft should be a model of mechanical perfection. You know the rules, but if you need a refresher course, try these guidelines:

- Use only elite or pica type. No script, italics, all-caps, dot matrix, or whatever happens to be trendy these days. Editors prefer pica but will read elite.
- In the upper left corner should be your name, complete address, and both day and evening phone numbers with area codes. In the upper right, put the approximate wordage and the rights you're offering for sale.
- Center the title of your article or short story halfway down on the first page. Always double-space, and use margins of about one and a fourth inches on all sides.
- On the upper left of every page after page one, type your last name and the page number.
- Don't staple the pages together, use a paperclip.

- Mail flat any manuscript of more than four pages. Fold in thirds manuscripts of four pages or less.
- Always include return postage and a self-addressed envelope.
- Keep a copy of the article for your files with the dates of submission and the market penciled on the top sheet.

Impress an editor with your extra care. Go over your final draft one last time before mailing it. Make minor corrections with a soft editing pencil. There is no need to retype as long as changes are made neatly and don't exceed three per page. Scratch any clichés that might have crept in, and substitute a common word for any obscure one that might require an editor to reach for his dictionary. Have you varied your sentence and paragraph length? Do you have enough dialogue? Quotes? Anecdotes?

Don't settle for a good word when a better one is out there begging to be pressed into service. Less is more at this point, so never spend two words when one will buy the same reaction. I'm reminded of an early writing teacher and author of a line of teenage adventure stories who once advised me to mentally turn my finished draft upside down and shake it until all clichés, redundancies, and overwritten phrases fall away, leaving nothing but pure prose.

Be prepared to support all statements made in your manuscript. If you've taped an interview or used questionnaires to gather information, hold them for several months after your article has been published. Such materials verify your research if the magazine or you are ever questioned.

Topping off your manuscript with a cover letter is optional. Unlike the query, this should be only about a half-page long and should reintroduce yourself and remind the editor that this is the manuscript he expressed an interest in seeing. In fact, I often send along a copy of his letter to jar his memory. To further assure that my manuscript gets to the right desk, I always write in the lower left-hand corner: "Requested Material."

ON A SCALE OF 1 TO 10, WHADDYA THINK?

Never, never expect a critique or evaluation of your manuscript. Editors simply don't have time. And speaking of time, impress an editor with your patience. Once you've mailed a manuscript, don't inquire on its status every other day. I know of several writers who always include postcards that say on the back: "Your manuscript has arrived at our office." The editor signs his name and drops it in the return mail.

How long should you play the waiting game? On a query, you can expect a reply within a month. For a magazine article, the average reporting time is six to eight weeks. For a book manuscript, it may be two to three months. A promising piece of writing is passed from first reader to second reader to third reader to fourth, and that takes time. Weeks. Even months. Don't force the issue by demanding an answer. If you haven't received any reply in two months, drop the editor a brief, cordial note. After all, there's always that obscure chance that the manuscript was lost in the mail or misplaced at the office. If that's the case, offer to send a copy.

Impress an editor by accepting his verdict. If you receive a flat rejection, don't challenge his judgment, plead, or badger him for a reason. If he suggests a rewrite, by all means do it. Realize that your words are not golden and they can be changed, perhaps for the better.

Finally, impress an editor with your resiliency. Whether your efforts were rejected at the query stage or the manuscript level, or whether your work was seriously considered and eliminated at the very end, don't cower in the corner and lick your wounds. Bounce back and try again. Don't become a closet writer. A favorite story of mine recounts a conversation between a young interviewer and Pearl Buck. Miss Buck was expressing some disappointment that an idea she had submitted for a short story had just been rejected by her publisher.

"You mean *you* get rejection slips?" marveled the beginner.

"Of course," said the Nobel Prize winner, smiling. "I'm a writer, aren't I?"

SUMMARY

Professionalism is an attitude. It's not tangible, but it's recognizable. It can't be bought, but it can be acquired. It has nothing to do with business cards decorated with quills and proclaiming the carrier a "wordsmith," or with watermarked stationery that lists affiliated writing organizations in raised printing. Professionalism is free. And rare.

Action Items

Less than two query letters out of ten result in sales. Resolve to improve those odds by submitting three article ideas based on topics close to home. Check the following resources and glean a salable idea from each. Have the letters in the mail by Friday.

1. Calendar.
   Turn your calendar ahead four months (remember that magazines work from three to six months in advance) and take note of specially marked holidays and observances. Concentrate on a less celebrated date and tie a timely topic to it. Example: "Post-Prom Party Ideas"; "Secretary's Day—Five Ways to Say 'Thanks' "; "Antique Gifts for the June Bride."

2. Map.
   Travel editors often complain that they receive too many queries on exotic destinations and not enough on out-of-the-way stateside attractions. What is your city's claim to fame? Bypass the museums, state forests, theme parks and other predictables. Choose a renovated grand hotel, an overlooked French restaurant, a historic stop on the underground railroad.

3. Hometown daily/weekly.
   Check your local newspaper for human interest items on colorful people doing colorful things. Note any conventions or professional meetings that will bring dozens of experts to town; don't overlook the classified section that will tout everything from yodeling lessons to rare breeds of cats.

Suggested Additional Readings

Writing with Style by Peter Jacobi (Chicago: Laurence Ragan Communications, Inc., 1982).

The Transitive Vampire by Karen Elizabeth Gordon (New York: Times Books, 1984).

The Writer's Quotation Book, edited by James Charlton (New York: Penguin Books, 1982).

3

Five Steps
to Writing a Salable
Article

The camera was a beauty: a 35mm SLR, fully automatic, with motor drive and complete with a 28–90 zoom lens. It was the missing link . . . nothing could hold her back now. First stop? New York, then Hartford and points north.

Her plan was simple: She would take leisurely trips to who-knows-where, scribble pithy reactions into a journal, snap a few photos, tape an interview or two, then return home to blend memories, souvenirs, and jottings into salable copy. While rates paid by travel magazines wouldn't catapult her into the next tax bracket, they'd surely underwrite the airfare and keep her in Ektachrome.

"So, what's your destination?" I asked enthusiastically.

"New England," she replied.

"And the story?"

"New England," she repeated.

We had a problem.

I convinced her that all six New England states would be difficult to capture in 2,000 words or less, and a multipart series with segments entitled "Rhode Island," "Connecticut," "New Hampshire," etc., would spark little more than a yawn from the staff over at *Endless Vacation*. We finally settled on three ideas—"Treasure-Hunting for Antiques in Northern Maine," "The Five Best Seafood Restaurants on Cape Cod," and "The Country Inns of Western Vermont"—and I sent her packing.

APPLAUSE, APPLAUSE

As a writer, I do a lot of networking with other writers. We applaud each other's successes, commiserate on defeats, and swap a fair share of advice. We love stories with happy endings, especially if the wrap-up line is provided by an editor and includes such words as "yes," "first rights," and "the check is in the mail." Whether the story is mine or belongs to one of my pals, I like to dissect a sale and try to determine why one manuscript earns kudos and the next only vetoes. Here's what I've learned. . . .

The writing process can be broken down into five steps: Coming up with a great idea; distilling it to coverline proportions; deciding on a slant; doing primary and secondary research; and then, of course, actually putting words to paper. Each step is essential, none expendable, and if followed without detour, each should lead to a freelance sale.

But don't spend that check yet. The process can stall out at any point, and getting back on course is impossible without starting again from the point of departure. My camera-toting friend, for instance, had failed to narrow her topic and would have filled her notebook with superficial generalizations about New England if we hadn't tightened her focus. Her research would have been faulty and a return trip would have been necessary to right the wrong. By identifying a specific geographic area and homing in on one aspect of the region, she was able to direct her camera and her thoughts toward a pertinent and picturesque subject. With some hustle on her part she could generate at least three salable articles . . . and that translates into a lot of Ektachrome.

TRACKING THE TIMELY TOPIC

Every writing project, fiction or nonfiction, begins with a carefully defined idea that's time has come, not come and gone. I'm always leery of the writer who complains he can't think of good topics. Most writers admit to the opposite problem—they can't turn off the idea spigot; the flow is so persistent that unless the ideas are poured into a journal, they may be overcome by the next wave.

"When I finish a book I go through a period of mourning, only it's not that dramatic," prolific novelist Suzanne Guntrum told me once during an interview. "I have to let the book and the characters go; only after my editor has read the manuscript and said everything is fine can I release it and let it fade away. In the meantime, I've got the next character in my mind and she starts coming forward. I've got enough material in my head now to last about four years. Actually, I have too many sets of characters in there waiting their turn. It's confusing."

Where do you look for an idea that's time has come? You use your ears more than your eyes. Listen to what people around you are talking about. Remember, readers care first and foremost about themselves; they want to read about topics that touch them. They want timely topics, not tired ones, self-help articles that will show them how to be smarter, richer, thinner, prettier, more successful, and better liked. They care about health (*their* health), sports (*their* teams), travel (destinations *they* can afford), religion, sex, humor, fitness, and self-preservation. The proof is on the best-seller list, past and present: *Looking Out for Number One, How to Have Thin Thighs in Thirty Days, Fit for Life, The Be (Happy) Attitudes, A Passion for Excellence.* See the trend?

If clues to people's cares are found in conversation, poll your own concerns. After all, you're a reader as well as a writer. What would you be most likely to read? Articles about money? Home computers? Decorating? Coping with divorce? How to ask your boss for a raise? Chances are, if these subjects interest you, they'll interest others, too.

Charles Kuralt once said that he steals some of his best ideas. When he was junketing across the country looking for poignant and witty P.S.s for the CBS Evening News shows, he always used local newspapers as sources. Often buried on the back pages of a small-town weekly he'd find tiny news items that briefly brought to the forefront people with unusual hobbies, habits, and hang-ups. Clip and save, advises Kuralt. The next time your flow of ideas slows to a trickle, look at the clips for inspiration. Currently in my follow-up file are blurbs about: a woman who writes letters to famous people and has built up a collection of replies from all major entertainment figures plus most international heads of state; a group of college kids who are trying to teeter-totter their way into the

Guinness Book; a convicted murderer, serving concurrent life sentences, who just completed his college degree and is entering law school via correspondence.

Sometimes the best ideas are right under our noses but we fail to recognize them because we're too close. I learned this the hard way. A few years ago, my hometown boasted the dubious distinction of having the highest unemployment rate in the country. It was higher than it had been during the Great Depression, but no soup lines were in evidence, no jobs programs had workers swabbing city streets, no one was sleeping on park benches. I didn't recognize the situation as a national story until the national media descended on us. *The Wall Street Journal* came to town, *Newsweek, Look, Fortune* followed. Their reporters were asking questions like, "Is the crime rate up? How are people coping? Are they reneging on church pledges? Are they leaving town? Are a lot of houses for sale?"

Good questions. Questions *I* should have been asking.

THINK SMALL

Even after you've identified an idea as being both scintillating and salable, you're not done. Have you narrowed it enough? Give it the coverline test (a *coverline* is merely those few words on the cover of a magazine that promote an article inside): Try to capsulize your idea in three or four words. If you can do it, you're ready to proceed with research. If not, indulge in a little distillation.

Example: The Indianapolis 500-Mile Race is the Main Event in the Hoosier capital on Memorial Day. A quarter of a million fans throng to the speedway, and scores of writers try to capture the color for readers. Yet, as many articles that have been written about "the greatest spectacle in racing," I've never seen one called, simply, "The Indianapolis 500-Mile Race." Impossible. Even the most talented writer couldn't hope to describe all the facets of the month-long activity. The focus must be narrowed, with dozens of stories resulting. Over the years, I've written auto-race-related articles called "Preacher of the Pits" (profile of a guitar-strumming evangelist who fancies himself spiritual leader of the race-car fraternity), "Bloody Good Show" (feature on the United States Auto Club's

British-born statistician), and "Fashion Picks for the 500" (interview with Indiana's own haute couturier, Halston).

One more "for instance": I once was part of a group of travel writers touring Disney World in search of off-beat features. Everyone was faced with the same dilemma: It's impossible to write the definitive article on the phenomenon called Disney World, yet what aspect of it hasn't been reported ad nauseam? Somehow, by narrowing our focus, each of us managed to uncover an original element. One woman wrote about "Keeping the Magic Kingdom in Bloom"—a behind-the-scenes tour of Disney greenhouses; another writer called his story "Not For Children Only"—a report on Disney World as a destination for senior citizens. I pursued "What to Do the *Second* Day"—side trips to enjoy *after* the predictable first day at the theme park.

GET MY DRIFT?

Before embarking on research, you need to decide the slant, or angle, of your article for the same reason that you need a glass to hold water—to keep your idea from spilling in several different directions. Even a tightly defined topic can be approached from a variety of angles, each unique, each requiring different research material.

A newspaper feature writer I know once took a phone call from a local schoolteacher who suggested the writer do a story on him.

"Why?" asked my friend, a man of few words.

"Because I just lost a hundred and fifteen pounds," replied the teacher. "And my wife went on the same diet and lost a hundred and twenty."

My friend was immediately interested. He saw the story as an excellent human interest feature for the hometown daily and also a possible freelance article for a national magazine. After all, everyone likes a slim-down, shape-up tale with a happy-ever-after ending. But before he arranged the interviews, he needed to decide what tack he wanted to take. He needed to know his direction. If his purpose was to inform readers, he'd merely tell the couple's story in straight news fashion; if he wanted to instruct, he'd need to include lots of advice—"How to Lose 235 Pounds in Six Months."

If he wanted to entertain, he'd need to elicit a variety of anecdotes about how students didn't recognize the couple, how the duo had nothing to wear, how their family reacted to them. If he wanted to recycle the material for a women's magazine, he'd need to emphasize how the weight loss put pizzazz into their marriage. If a fitness magazine was his objective, he'd have to concentrate on the exercise program that worked in tandem with the Weight Watcher diet. If *Psychology Today* was his destination, he'd steer discussion to the effects of the weight loss. Did the couple respect each other more? Was renewed self-confidence a byproduct of the diet? What mental games did they play with each other to keep their willpower from fading?

By knowing the angle he wished to pursue, my friend was able to get exactly the information he needed without circling the issue, wasting time, and gathering superfluous quotes he'd have to transcribe from his tape and wade through in the transcript.

DIG, DIG, DIG

Research comes in two packages—secondary and primary. Secondary source research involves going to the library and becoming thoroughly up to date on what's been written about your topic by other writers. It means using the *Reader's Guide to Periodical Literature*, the card catalogue, reference books, and even microfilm. If you find a good book, check it out; if you locate a helpful article, make a copy. Otherwise, take notes, lots of notes.

Don't make the mistake of thinking you have to be an expert on every topic you tackle. If this were the case, not much would be written today. Often, it's better *not* to be too knowledgeable when you begin. Then you are on the same level as your readers and will ask the same questions they would ask if given the opportunity. Over the years, I've written articles on politicians I didn't believe in, a church denomination I don't belong to, a rare disease I didn't understand (neither did the doctors), country music, opera, the national budget, and circus clowns. I didn't know very much about any of them when I started, but I learned. I'm trainable. And so are you.

Doing primary research is when the fun starts. It's legwork: getting involved with your topic, and even participating in it. It means uncovering information that has never been written before—talking to people, interviewing experts, pulling in your own experience, observing events and sources, even playing George Plimpton and jumping into the action. When I wrote a book about body building, I pumped iron; when I did a series on spiritualism, I attended a séance or two; when I researched an article on hot-air ballooning, I became half of a two-person crew that floated over the countryside at dawn.

Many beginning writers are nervous about collecting primary research. Don't be. Experts love to talk about their interests and are flattered to be asked advice. Every university, hospital, industrial complex, and governmental agency employs P.R. (public relations) specialists whose job is to provide information, set up interviews, and help writers gather facts. They're being paid to help you. Take advantage of their services.

PULLING IT ALL TOGETHER

Since writing is more a "show me" than a "tell me" business, let's apply the five steps of writing an article to a real writing situation and see how they resulted in a sale.

The editor of *Indianapolis Magazine* once called me and said she wanted "something about fall fashion" for her September issue. "Wait a minute," I replied, "I'm no expert on clothes, and besides, I don't care much about. . ."

My protests turned to lukewarm acceptance when the editor, a friend, explained the idea had come from the publisher at the last minute and, thus, was elevated to "must run" status. Could I bail her out? Put that way, how could I refuse?

First stop was the local library when I flipped through current fashion magazines in an effort to pick up on trends, jot down a few observations, and note the names of well-known designers. The topic had to be narrowed, of course, and after being overwhelmed by the anything-goes mind-set of the female fashion industry (hemlines are up, hemlines are down, bold colors are in, bold colors are out), I decided men's styles posed less of a problem. Since my assignment came from a city magazine, regional boundaries further limited my topic. By the time I left the library, I had decided my article would look at fall wardrobe picks for Indianapolis men on the move. I had also taken the first two steps in the article-writing process: I had been given a timely idea (fashion), and I had narrowed it down (by season, by region, by sex).

Because fashion is such a current topic, I knew I'd have to depend on primary, not secondary, research. I had to identify some "experts" who would be willing to share their knowledge of the marketplace with me. I asked several area businessmen to tell me which local clothing store they considered the best. The name that received the most votes was a small chain with headquarters in Kalamazoo. I called and asked to speak with the man in charge of buying. As it turned out, he was a good source; he assured me he was also the owner, business manager, director of advertising, and in a pinch, he'd sweep the floors. Was he willing to talk? You bet. Remember, he doubled as advertising director and this article promised to be read by his target audience. He boasted that his Indianapolis outlet was by far his most successful, and he seemed happy to comment on clothing tastes of area men (conservative), what would be fashionable for fall (classics), and what he advised for "investment" purchases (herringbones, Harris tweeds, et al.).

Although he was a credible source, another expert's point of view was needed to add depth to my article. I studied the ads in the *Indianapolis Star* and was delighted to read that Brooks Brothers, the stodgy old New York clothier, was preparing to open a branch at a posh local shopping mall. This was the source I needed, I thought—East Coast chic—so I called the New York headquarters and was put in touch with the vice-president in charge of marketing. Did he have a few minutes? I asked. Of course he did, he responded, especially when he realized I represented a city magazine read by his new branch's potential customers.

My research file was growing, but I needed a slant. If only I could find a Big Name who could comment not just on fashion trends but on long-term style. I wanted a Star, but he'd have to have some local tie since this was a regional publication. Wishful thinking? Maybe so, but I headed back to the library and scanned *Who's Who* in search of a famous designer with Indianapolis roots.

"Bill Blass," I reported to my editor by phone the next day. "He's from Fort Wayne, but that's only a hundred miles from Indy."

"Close enough," she agreed.

Several calls later I spoke with Blass's public relations director who scheduled a phone interview with Blass for the following morning. I used the time to go back to the library and do extensive research on the world-famous designer. Among the facts I uncovered was his date of birth. I realized that just about the time the issue would hit the newsstands, Blass would be marking his sixtieth birthday. There was my slant: "In an anniversary year, Hoosier-born designer Bill Blass reflects on style, past, present and future." The other two interviews could be combined into a sidebar about best fall fashion buys for Indianapolis men.

Postscript: Blass was pleased with the attention from his home state's media, talked enthusiastically about his career, and shared preview photos of his fall collection of men's clothing. Somehow the little fashion feature that I hadn't wanted to do emerged as the cover story of the September issue and brought an extra bonus from a satisfied publisher and a "thank you" from a bailed-out editor.

SUMMARY

Nothing is impossible for a resourceful writer, or at least for a writer with good sources. Before you reject an idea as impossible to pursue, walk through the five-step process and surmount obstacles one at a time. If you've come up with a good idea, narrowed it, decided on a slant, and identified good sources, the final step—the writing part—should be the easiest of all.

Action Items

1. List five general article ideas you would like to pursue.

2. Narrow your ideas until you can "capture" each in a four- to five-word coverline.

3. Plot your research. Whom would you need to interview? What facts would you need to uncover?

4. How could each article best be illustrated (photos, drawings, charts, graphs)?

5. Come up with two possible markets for each article idea.

Suggested Additional Readings

Writing for Your Readers by Donald Murray (Chester, Connecticut: The Globe Pequot Press, 1983).

Language Skills for Journalists by R. Thomas Berner (Boston: Houghton Mifflin Company, 1984).

Interviews That Work by Shirley Biagi (Belmont, California: Wadsworth Publishing Company, 1986).

Free-lancer and Staff Writer by William L. Rivers and Alison R. Work (Belmont, California: Wadsworth Publishing Company, 1986).

4

Becoming Prolific and Profitable

The secret to success in any business, including freelance writing, is not to work harder but to work smarter.

Working smarter as a freelancer means getting the most mileage from one manuscript or writing idea as you possibly can.

This can be achieved through *cyclical marketing*, wherein you sell your same Christmas articles (or vacation or Easter or spring cleaning articles) once each year. It can also be done by *series writing*, in which you sell a series of articles on one topic and then later combine them to create a book. These are just two of the marketing strategies we will examine in this chapter.

Smarter marketing will increase your profit margin. To increase it even more, you'll have to learn to be prolific. That calls for turning out a lot of words, and it can be done painlessly if you learn some of the basic speed-writing procedures used by successful freelancers. Let's examine that first.

WRITING ARTICLES IMPROMPTU

Baseball teams have "utility" men and newspapers have "magicians."

At least that's what I call them. A magician is a reporter who in twenty minutes can change five bulging files about pollution into a superb 800-word sidebar or a 1,500-word feature.

Me? It used to take me that long to come up with a good lead.

Back in 1975, when I was a part-time reporter for the *Muncie Star*, I was baffled by the speed at which these magicians could churn out copy when pressed by a deadline. I wanted to learn how to do that sort of presto–change-o act myself.

So I attached myself to a veteran magician named George, and I became a journalistic sorcerer's apprentice. I studied hard and before long I was able to speed write with the best of them. Our editor would say, "Here's our file on state lotteries. Give me a thousand words on the chances of one getting started here in Indiana. I need it in half an hour." And twenty-seven minutes later, I'd have the piece written, typed, and laid on his desk.

Like all great magicians, my mentor George had a bag of tricks to teach me. He explained that the knack to becoming an impromptu writer was being able to select an appropriate writing format and then to isolate all the information that could fit that format. The rest you ignored.

"Let's say, for example, that the editor hands you a fat file with dozens of tearsheets and clippings in it on the subject of street cleaning," explained George, "and he tells you that the local street cleaners have gone on strike. He then assigns you to do a short piece of seven hundred and fifty words on what impact the strike could have on the city. You've got thirty minutes to write it. What are you going to do?"

"Wring my hands and cry?" I suggested.

"No, no," said George. "All you need to do is choose the most appropriate format, find the clippings that apply to it, pull out the best statistics and quotes from that material, organize everything, and type it."

That sounded logical. That is, if I only knew the formats. I asked George to tell them to me. He did; they worked "like magic"; and now I'm going to show them to you. Each format has an overview topic and then a series of specific questions used to organize and explain it.

Format 1: *Pro and Con Arguments*
- What is positive about this thing? (Price? Style? Prestige?)
- What is negative about it? (Cost? Repairs? Noise? Tackiness?)
- Which outweighs the other?

- What recommendations or predictions are people making?

Format 2: *Short- and Long-Range Views*
- What can we expect of this thing this year?
- Which trends will it set or follow this decade?
- How can people weather its ups and downs?
- Which generation will pay for it and which will benefit from it?

Format 3: *Past and Present Circumstances*
- What is the history of this matter?
- What are its most recent developments?
- How does the matter now stand?
- Why must this matter be resolved now?

Format 4: *Similarities and Differences*
- In what ways are the two things alike in regard to cost, customs, age, clientele, setting, or other pertinent factors?
- In what ways are they different, dissimilar, or opposite?
- Which of the two is preferable or more advantageous?

Format 5: *Major and Minor Concerns*
- In what ways will this event greatly alter standard procedure?
- What life-style changes, physical moves, or cash outlays will occur?
- What minor details have been overlooked?
- What concerns have been overrated, exaggerated, or amplified?

Format 6: *Endorsements and Condemnations*
- Who is in favor of it? Why? How strongly will they support it?
- Who is against it? Why? What can they do to thwart it?
- What position papers have been issued concerning the matter?
- Which way is the public leaning in this matter?

Once you become familiar with these formats, you just need to select the one that best applies to your topic at hand and then organize your research accordingly.

Most active freelance writers build personal home file systems by clipping daily newspaper articles and monthly magazine articles and then filing them under generic topics such as, "Art," "Children," "Money," "Religion," "Sports," "Travel," and so on. If they join a writers' club, these files are multiplied in the sense that one writer can get on the phone to a fellow club member and say, "Hey, Marge, can I borrow that file you've built up on local historic landmarks? I want to put together a sidebar for a magazine piece I'm doing on Presidents' Day."

Public and university libraries often also have files filled with pamphlets, flyers, bulletins, press releases, and other nonbook materials that relate to a specific topic. Usually these may not be checked out, but may be used in the library. These materials are especially helpful to freelance writers who write weekly columns for local newspapers and need to report on current events.

Sifting and Sorting

The work of pulling pertinent material from the file is a rather routine chore once you select the proper format.

In George's example of an article on the impact of a street cleaners' strike, Format 5, "Major and Minor Concerns," would probably be most appropriate. In sifting through the file of clippings, you could discard any items about the personal lives of street cleaners, how to repair a street cleaning vehicle, or what street cleaners do in the off season to amuse themselves. What you *will* be looking for will be items on street cleaner unions, wages, and benefits; the city's annual street cleaning bill; recent demands by street cleaners; and frequency of street cleanings on various routes.

You now use this material to answer the questions associated with Format 5. It might look like this:

How . . . alter standard procedure?
- Citizens will have to clean their own streets.
- Parades in town must be postponed.
- Sewer drains will become clogged; streets may flood.

Changes . . . moves . . . cash outlays?
- Poorer neighborhoods may develop health hazards.
- Roads may deteriorate faster.

- Debris laden streets may cause auto accidents.

Minor details . . . overlooked?
- Who will pull maintenance on unused street cleaning vehicles?

What concerns . . . overrated?
- Is street cleaning really as "stressful" as the union insists?
- Does the city really need an "emergency" street cleaning unit?

At first you may want to jot notes, as in the previous example. As you use the system more, you'll be able to organize it in your head or simply by spreading out the reference articles before you in the sequence you'll need to refer to them. If material has been published in a newspaper, it is public domain and can be reused by you. If material is taken from a copyrighted magazine article, you can give credit by saying "as reported in *Savvy.*"

Impromptu writing techniques are extremely useful to freelance columnists, staff reporters, feature writers who use sidebars, editors who need to produce filler copy, and publishers of newsletters. It's easy to master because it follows a set pattern of research and writing.

In fact, I've just proved that I am a *magician*. By reading this section of this chapter, you've been changed into an impromptu writer.

Abracadabra! Gotcha.

FICTION MADE EASIER

While I'm on the subject of the writing techniques I learned when working as a reporter, let me share with you a journalistic approach to creating fictional characters.

My training in newspaper reporting, magazine interviewing, and book researching has focused my career heavily on nonfiction. Nevertheless, I enjoy writing fiction; and I've discovered that my training in journalistic investigative procedures can be applied to creating believable fictional characters. Let me explain.

Whenever a news story breaks, reporters scramble to discover and report on the five Ws and the H: Who, what, when, where, why, and how (and, usually, how much, too).

Later, after this surface news has been reported, feature writers are then assigned to get an in-depth understanding of the full story. For example, if the surface news is that the mayor has resigned, the feature writers will find out what impact this will have on the mayor's political party, how the mayor's family feels about the situation, who convinced the mayor to act now, what people's opinions of the mayor are, and what options are still open for the mayor's political future.

In short, the feature writer will try to make the feature story lively and intriguing by first making the profiled person seem humanly three-dimensional and then making the associated news event seem important and timely. This will be done by answering four critical questions:

1. What are the circumstances of the news event?
2. What is the person's background?
3. What does the person look like?
4. What was the person's motive?

Good fictional characters can be developed by answering the same questions. After all, fictional characters have to *seem* real to readers. So let's review the above four questions in that light.

Circumstances

We know that without plot conflict (circumstances) there can be no story. As such, your fictional character must be placed into a situation of stress. This is not difficult since there are only nine fundamental plot conflicts for you to choose from:

- Man against himself
- Man against man
- Man against God
- Man against nature/environment
- Man against predetermined fate
- Man against the unknown

- Man against machine
- Man against society/culture
- Man against predicaments (being fired; contracting a disease, etc.)

Having selected a generic topic, you then need only to narrow it to something specific within that range. If, for example, you select *man against machine,* you may wish to write a sad story about an elderly crossing guard who is replaced by a stoplight, or a crime story about a computer thief who tries to crack computerized corporate payroll systems. The options and variations are limitless.

Background

You next need to fabricate a detailed dossier on your main character(s). Where was he or she born, educated, employed? Which parent, sibling, teacher, friend, or relative had a major influence on this person? What political party, religious sect, branch of military service, and labor union does this person belong to?

Although detailing these facts is a bit time-consuming, it's much quicker than having to dig up all these facts about a real person. Besides, it's fun. You get to create a person from scratch.

The dossier gives you a permanent record of each of your characters so that each person is consistent in looks and behavior throughout your work of fiction. A character cannot have a tattoo on his left arm in chapter one and then have the tattoo on his right arm in chapter seven. Each dossier also helps you to delineate your characters by purposely not making them all redheads or all twenty-year-old college students or all ex-Marines.

I have a "Personality Profile" sheet that I use as a research guide whenever I am hired to do a magazine profile of someone (see sidebar). I use this same sheet whenever I am creating a fictional character.

Naturally, only one tenth of the information in the profile will ever get mentioned in your story. That's not important. What *is* important is that you will know your character thoroughly and your character will be realistic. What *does* get mentioned in your story about the character will truly be important for the reader to know.

Appearance

Your third step will be to "see" what your character looks like. Whenever I am getting ready to interview a famous person, I obtain several pictures of that person (from magazines, P.R. agents, high school and college yearbooks). I study the eyes, the expressions, the posture. This gives me a "sense" of the person even before we meet.

You should do the same thing with your fictional characters. Carefully review the facts in your dossiers and then thumb through magazines, mail order catalogues, brochures, and pamphlets until you find models or actors or other people whose pictures are flesh-and-blood manifestations of your fictional characters.

Cut out these pictures and mount them on a "character board" (bulletin board) across from your writing desk. Put each character's name in bold letters below his or her picture. Now your characters not only have histories, they also have faces. They are real . . . at least to you and your readers.

The more you look at your characters, the more lifelike they will seem to you. Marilyn Durham kept a life-sized poster of actor Lee Van Cleef in her writing room the whole time she was writing her western novel, *The Man Who Loved Cat Dancing*. It was her visual model for her main character. (Ironically, Burt Reynolds got the part in the movie version.) In character development, seeing does lead to believing . . . and knowing . . . and enhancing.

Motive

Your final step is to develop motives for what your characters will be doing. In an investigative journalism assignment, if I am trying to figure out why a real-life person behaved the way he did, I go back to the data I've obtained for the Personality Profile sheet. Then I ask myself, Why did this man abuse his wife? According to my research, I am reminded, his father had beaten his mother regularly. Perhaps the younger man was conditioned to disrespect spouses. There's the motive: like father, like son.

Your fictional dossiers will give you similar ideas for character

Personality Profile Sheet

Person's full legal name:
Date of birth:
Place of birth:
Father's occupation:
Mother's occupation:
Brothers' names and birth
 dates:
Sisters' names and birth dates:
Famous or important relatives:
Family pets:
Father's philosophy of life/work:
Mother's philosophy of life/
 work:
Lessons learned from parents:
Childhood friends and
 neighbors:
Childhood escapades, hobbies,
 accidents:
Grade school name, location,
 and years attended
 A. Favorite teachers
 B. Favorite subjects
 C. Noteworthy incidents
High school name, location, and
 years attended
 A. Type of classes
  (vocational? college
  prep?)
 B. Sports participated in
 C. Scholastic honors
 D. Extracurricular
  activities
College names, locations, and
 years attended
 A. Degrees, majors, and
  minors
 B. Vocational goals

Height:
Weight:
Color of eyes:
Color of hair:
General health:
Gestures, mannerisms:
Tone of voice:
Facial expressions:
Manner of dress:
Size and appearance:
Demeanor:
Office surroundings
 A. Desktop photos
 B. Wall hangings
 C. Room decor
Job title and responsibilities:
Personal triumphs and failures:
Outstanding achievements:
Pet peeves:
Career turning points:
Daily routine:
Leisure activities:
Hobbies:
Clubs, civic groups:
Religious beliefs:
Political leanings:
Reading preference:
Avocations:
Arts enjoyed: (music? dance?
 sculpture?)
Future plans:
Things he wishes he had done
 differently:
Philosophy of life/business:
World travels:

(Continued)

Personality Profile Sheet (*continued*)

    C. Sports and
        extracurricular
        activities
    D. Scholarships, grants,
        honors, awards
    E. Part-time and/or
        summer jobs
  Military background
    A. Years of service and
        branch
    B. Highest held rank
    C. Medals, decorations,
        campaigns
  Family background
    A. Courtship, marriage
    B. Children, home life

---

behavior patterns and motives. Keep in mind that your main characters have to solve their own problems, since that makes a plot.

Your character must be motivated by something all-consuming (greed, ambition, fame, power, revenge) so that whatever he or she creates or solves or changes or attacks or steals or fights against to the last ounce of strength will seem logical within the context of the story. For example, you and I wouldn't have gotten into the ring against Muhammad Ali at his peak for all the gold in Fort Knox (pure suicide). However, in a similar situation, we *do* believe that Rocky Balboa would go against Apollo Creed (a similar suicide mission) because the author has convinced us that, win or lose, here is a guy who must at least take his shot at the championship. It's completely believable *within the context* of that story.

You must also allow your character to have a life of his own. If your pen surprises you with some unusual plot twists and character motives, go with the flow awhile. See what happens.

Once, an author was approached at a party by an angry woman. "Sir!" she exclaimed. "I have just finished reading your latest novel. I simply could not believe it when that beautiful eighteen-year-old princess ran off with that seventy-two-year-old baron."

"I assure you, madam," replied the author, "I was as shocked as you were."

All writers have a mental file cabinet filled with memories of unusual characters they have encountered in life. If you can tap these memories, organize them into dossiers, and find faces to match them, you'll have several three-dimensional characters on your hands. Thereafter, it's just a matter of asking yourself, "How would this person react if confronted by a dead body . . . or an escaped prisoner . . . or a sudden bankruptcy . . . or the birth of triplets . . . or an unexpected scholarship?"

And you'll know the answers. After all, they're *your* people.

USING ALL DRAFTS

Once the characters are established for your novel, you'll have to experiment with plot ideas. What will these characters be doing that will fascinate a reader enough to keep him or her turning pages?

Usually, your first and second drafts of certain stories, articles, or chapters that you develop will not satisfy you. That's fine. It's important to get your story down on paper first and then to revise it later. Holly Miller and I write novels together under the pen name of Leslie Holden, and we have been known to rewrite a chapter as many as five times before it "says" what we need it to say.

Have you ever had that same problem?

In revising and editing the first draft of something you've written, have you ever had to cut a scene or passage you especially liked?

Who hasn't, eh? Wow, that hurts.

But for the sake of the total story, you always do cut it. The passage was good, but just not appropriate. Zing! Into the trash can it goes.

But wait! . . . You're making a mistake!

It's good to edit your material carefully and to delete any inappropriate passages, but it's foolish to throw away any piece of fine writing. There's a very good chance you may be able to use it somewhere else sometime. As an example of this, let me tell you a true incident from literary history which may surprise you.

You probably have read Jack London's classic short story, "To Build a Fire." It's included in most high school and college literature books. The story was published in *Century* magazine in 1908 and has since been reprinted many other places. It relates the shocking tale of a Yukon prospector who freezes to death after slipping through ice. The man's numb hands are unable to build a fire. The story is compelling, graphic, and haunting. It's a true masterpiece of short fiction.

But guess what? That masterpiece had its foundation in the discarded scraps of an earlier London story.

Unknown to most people, Jack London published a different story called "To Build a Fire" in *Youth's Companion* back on May 29, 1902. This version was shorter and less sophisticated (and in it the prospector did not freeze to death). London had been told that stories with "sad endings" would not sell, so he cut all harsh scenes from the first version and marketed it as a children's story.

But he held on to his original ideas. Five years later, as an established author, he wrote the version of the story he had really wanted to write. It proved to be a stunning piece of writing.

Now, how about you? What have you thrown away lately that might instead have been turned into a masterpiece? Makes you wonder, doesn't it?

Salvage Operation

Knowing what actually should be discarded and what should be saved is not always easy to determine. Most active writers have learned to be disciplined at self-editing. It takes practice, but it can be mastered in fairly short order. There are only a few procedures to follow:

- Delete any off-the-track or tangential passages.
- Make sure all transitions are smooth.
- Double-check spelling, grammar, and typing.
- Rewrite any scenes or passages of dialogue that are predictable.
- Read the story aloud to test for pace and continuity.

• Make sure that all copy either moves the action forward or provides essential information.

Famed editor Maxwell Perkins wrote to Morley Callahan in 1931, "When one writes a story he does not put everything in, but selects with a view to the motive of the story. The details he uses are those which are significant in the light of the motive."

Most writers know this. That's why they aren't afraid to cut. That's essential to self-editing.

But as good as they are at cutting, most writers are quite inept at salvaging good copy. Most haven't the slightest idea of what to do with an "extra" scene or two pages of unused dialogue or three paragraphs of superfluous statistical research.

The answer is to employ the five Rs: retain, reslant, revise, review, and resell.

Retain everything you've had to cut. Hold it in a folder for at least six months. Read it from time to time to keep your subconscious mind aware of it. As ideas pop up for possible uses of the salvaged segments, make notes to yourself about them on the cover of the folder.

As you brainstorm, ask yourself how a *reslanting* of the original article, along with the insertion of written segments you previously cut, might help create a new article. For example, if your first version was geared toward men, perhaps your new version could be slanted toward women readers. If the previous version was for juveniles, maybe the new version could be made to appeal to senior citizens.

Another way to reslant the article is to take something you previously deleted and to use it now as your new perspective lead. For example, your first version may have focused on *people* who design and make quilts. To keep the article on track, you deleted all paragraphs that explained how to make quilts. Now, however, in your new version, you could slant the article toward a *how-to* format and use data about people simply as filler or local color for your new article.

You can go right through standard journalistic procedures in reslanting an article. The first article could emphasize the "who" of the topic; the second article could emphasize the "what"; the third article the "when"; and so on until you've covered "where," "why," "how," and "how much." This gives you seven totally different slants and enables you to make use of virtually any scraps of previously deleted copy.

Previous Decisions

Revising an article can also create new openings for unused copy. Pull out your first draft and go back through it. Delete 25 percent of what you've written. For a 3,000-word feature, you'll have to cut 750 words; usually you'll cut general background information, certain descriptive passages, and perhaps some dialogue. Now, insert 750 words of previously unpublished copy about the topic. Give your article a new lead, some quotes from different people, and a few interesting statistics. With these brushstrokes, you'll have a new article.

Another way to revise is to bring your article up to date. Call your previous sources and ask about late-breaking developments, the latest statistics and facts, new quotes, new predictions, new views, new circumstances. Take these new elements, combine them with material you had no room for in the original version, and write a "new" article about something that is "old hat" to you.

Another revision procedure is to organize all of your deleted passages that deal with sensory elements and use them so that the reader "experiences" the topic: Instead of an impersonal *report* on the topic, offer a vivid presentation of the sounds, smells, tastes, sights, and tactile sensations associated with skydiving or mudwrestling or garden planting or whatever your topic may be. You'll be basing everything on all your original research, but your writing will be completely new.

A final revision tip is to give your first draft to another writer or editor and ask, "How do you think this could have been better?" When the responses come back ("More quotes from expert sources" . . . "The old mansion should have been described more clearly" . . . "It needs some humor") you can go to your folder of "cut" passages and pull out whatever is needed.

Your file folder will soon be bulging with the numerous reslantings and revisions of your original article. It will then be time to *review* carefully all of your material. As you review, ask yourself these questions:

- Do I now have enough material on this topic to form the basis for a book, pamphlet, or lecture series that could generate extra income for me?
- Could my material be rewritten for a different medium, such as a business training film (screenplay) or a cassette tape series (audio script)?

If your review leads you to believe there's a potential "afterlife" in a new medium for your published articles (lectures, films, tapes, books), develop a proposal, contact an editor, and *resell* your material.

And as you begin revising for the new markets, don't throw away anything you cut. Remember, it's all grist for the next trip to the mill.

CYCLICAL MARKETING

All right, now that you are convinced that you should save and use material that has not as yet been published, let's take the next step in the process and learn how to save and reuse material that *has* been published. This is known as cyclical marketing of standard articles.

Once each year I really get on my wife's nerves. Rose is usually a loving wife and, for a fact, the best secretary I've ever had. But I know I've really pushed her to the limit when (usually around February) I hear her groan from her office, "Oh, no! Not *this* thing again. Aggghhh!"

The source of her agony is a manuscript of mine called, "How to Be an Effective Listener." Since 1978, I have sold that article to *Plus 60 Magazine, The Florida Real Estate Professional's Journal, Market Builder, Pace, Fort Wayne Today, Roto, New Cleveland Woman Journal, Editor's Workshop, Optical Management,* and to six newspapers. It also has appeared as part of my book *Uncommon Sense: Fueling Success Skills with Enthusiasm* (R & R Newkirk, 1984).

And guess who helped me proofread it every time it was submitted somewhere? That's right: my wife, partner, and secretary, Rose. The only thing that has preserved our sanity over the years is the knowledge that this one article has earned us thousands of dollars. (That's not to say, however, that we weren't overjoyed when word processors came along and feature articles could be stored on disks and only the revisions in the article had to be retyped.) Remarketing favorite topics is a standard operational procedure of both writers and editors. Knowing about this can make you seem prolific, as well as make your freelance marketing efforts very profitable.

Faithful Old Standards

When King Solomon proclaimed three thousand years ago that there was nothing new under the sun, he wasn't referring to magazine articles . . . but he could have been. The fact is, if you were to examine the back issues of the nation's leading magazines, you would discover that they have been covering the same topics over and over at regular intervals. True, the titles are different and so are the authors, but seldom the subjects.

The reason editors repeat articles is because audiences change. One year, a young lady might subscribe to *Seventeen*; the next year, however, she'll switch to *Modern Bride*; the following year she's moved on to *Family Circle*. For a time, her brother will read *Boy's Life*; he then will switch to *Hot Rod*; he'll finally wind up with *Gentleman's Quarterly*. As each magazine's audience rotates, it falls to the editors to replay the article topics that have earned each magazine its particular audience.

As a freelancer, this becomes important marketing knowledge for you. By studying back issues of a magazine you wish to break into and thereby discovering its repetitive themes, you can project what its future rotational needs will be.

For example, let's assume that there is a magazine called *Big Time Investments* that pays 35 cents per word for articles. You want to make a sale there, so you go to the library and pull out the bound volumes of all editions of that magazine for the past six or seven years.

You begin to read the article titles in the tables of contents. As you do, you make a note of the generic topics it covers. Each time an issue runs an article about one of these topics, you make a check mark by it on your list (perhaps even noting the date it appeared).

At the end of your examination, your checklist perhaps reveals that *Big Time Investments* has run an article about diamonds every two years, an article about gold every eighteen months, an article about silver every year, an article about stocks every six months, and an article on real estate every other issue. So you've now discovered the hottest general topic for this magazine: real estate.

Next, you carefully make a list of eight or ten of the article titles that relate to real estate investments. You discover that three of the eight titles you've listed are these: "Buying Condos with No Downpayment"; "Full Financing for Rental Properties"; and "No Up-Front Cash for Eastern Land Tracts." This then tells you that the specific article topic that readers want covered most frequently is how to invest in real estate, even if one lacks initial investment capital.

Knowing this, you next read all articles that *Big Time Investments* has published on that topic during the past five years. You take good notes. It isn't hard. You've found a dozen different articles on that topic, but after you've read four of them, they've started to repeat themselves.

DEPENDABLE MAGAZINE TOPICS THAT APPEAR IN CYCLICAL INTERVALS

Career:	College, interviews, promotions, salary
Entertainment:	Athletics, hobbies, music, travel
Family:	Adoption, childbirth, the elderly, pregnancy
Fashion:	Colors, costs, designs, fabrics, trends
Food:	Cake designing, recipes, specialty desserts
Health:	Diets, exercise programs, sleep, vitamins
Love:	Dating, divorce, marriage, sex, widowhood
Money:	Estate planning, investments, savings, taxes
Politics:	Candidates, investigations, laws, lobbies
Religion:	Cults, media outreach, prophecy, sects

Having analyzed your notes for the basic material needed for such an article, your next move is to find some sort of new angle for representing it. There are three ways you go about this:

1. Get quotes from experts on this topic who have not previously been featured in that magazine.
2. Develop unique sidebars, different photographs, and specialized graphics, which give a "face lift" to this granddaddy topic's artistic layout in the magazine.
3. Make sure that your article contains virtually everything new (previously unpublished) about this topic, such as new laws or regulations, current research and studies, and/or recently reported case histories.

You submit your feature, the editor recognizes it as exactly the thing his readers want, and he purchases it from you. He also sends you a letter and asks, "Have you ever written anything about the stock market?"

Naturally you are only too eager to go back and discover what kind of stock market article has been most popular in *Big Time Investments* during the past five years. Once having discovered it, you prepare a new version of it, submit it, and once again please your editor.

Meanwhile, however, your original article (on no-downpayment real estate) has been published in *Big Time Investments*. Because you sold first rights only, you now own the article again. You take your carbon copy from your file drawer, revamp it a bit to meet the editorial style of *Get Rich Tabloid*, and send it off. It sells a second time and you are convinced that you've written a standard that will be an annual sale for you . . . for as long as you can stand to retype it.

In fact, it occurs to you that you may rewrite your own article under a pseudonym three years from now and sell it to *Big Time Investments* again.

DEVELOPING A SERIES

Throughout this chapter we have emphasized the importance of working smarter, not harder. We have seen how this can be done by saving everything you write, by making use of cyclical marketing, by writing according to the most appropriate format, and by writing in both the fiction and nonfiction fields.

Now, to draw all this together, we are going to see how to put a book together and market it to a publisher in the easiest possible way.

Of the two biggest challenges a freelancer faces, I believe marketing is far tougher than writing. For that reason, I have developed a successful marketing system that both lines up a string of advance sales *and* predetermines the kind of writing needed for those sales.

The system has three phases:

1. Develop and write a series of articles on a specific topic for a specific magazine.
2. Combine the series of articles and sell them as a book.
3. Sell excerpts from the published book.

I have written numerous books and all but one (a library reference book) began as a series of articles in one or more magazines. Let me take you step by step through the process I used in marketing my book *Staying Ahead of Time* (R & R Newkirk, 1981).

Step 1: *Look for a Multifaceted Topic.*
You first must find a topic of great interest to yourself and other readers. Make the topic diverse enough to be analyzed from many perspectives. In my case, I chose the topic of time management.

Step 2: *Prepare an Extensive Outline of Your Book.*
Decide what the structure of your nonfiction book will be. You will need chapters on the background of your subject, its case histories, past and current research on the topic, reviews of current literature written about it, interviews with experts in the field, and commentaries on innovations, new concepts and experiments related to this topic.

For my time management book I decided to have a unit on how people throughout the ages have measured, valued, and used time (background; case histories). I also decided to interview numerous successful business and civic leaders to find out the systems they used for managing time (interviews; commentaries; experiments; innovations). Finally, I determined to try to develop some new systems of my own (new concepts) and to prepare a suggested reading list (current literature) for the book's appendix.

Step 3: *Focus on Specific Problems.*
From your large overview topic, isolate one particular problem. In an article, discuss and solve the problem.

One small but nagging problem people told me they had in managing time was in knowing what to do with themselves during a long layover at an airport terminal. I prepared an article called "Overcoming Terminal Problems," which explained ten useful activities a person could do during a layover.

I sold the airport article as a freelance piece to *Roto* magazine in Indiana and then to *Gulfshore Life* in Florida. I sent tearsheets of both published articles to the editor of *Market Builder* magazine (a publication geared toward people in sales) and suggested a one-year, twelve-article series on time management.

The editor was impressed with the idea and said yes. She bought the reprint rights to the airport article as the first feature for the series. Bingo! I now had eleven future article sales guaranteed.

I continued to move through my book outline, finding more and more time management problems to solve or systems to report on. Each became a new feature article. I sent each original article to the editor of *Market Builder* and kept a photostat copy for my records.

My agreement with *Market Builder* specified three points: Each article was to be paid for upon acceptance; copyright ownership would rest with me, as author; and once each new article appeared in *Market Builder*, I was free to sell it anywhere else I chose.

I finished all twelve articles for the series in nine weeks and received full payment for them. During the next year, as each article appeared in *Market Builder*, I began to resell that feature to other markets (to provide bonus cash, plus additional byline exposure). A few modifications of the *Market Builder* features would redirect them to vacationers, senior citizens, students, or whatever the new markets might be.

Step 4: *Prepare Folders on the Topics.*
As you do research on the topics covered in your projected chapters,

keep all of your notes, printed features, and drafts of new articles
in separate folders labeled by each chapter title.

Step 5: *Write the Book's Chapters.*
With advance money in your pocket from the sale of your series,
as well as regular reprint sales being made each month, you can
take time out to write your book. Take all of the material in one of
your folders and form it into a chapter.

Take your published articles on that chapter's general topic and
link them together with subtitles, transitional anecdotes, and filler
sections. Flesh out your articles by adding more quotes (from your
interview notes), additional references, and footnotes. Enhance each
chapter by developing sidebars, charts, maps, graphs, quizzes, and/
or summaries that can be placed strategically throughout the pages.

For my time management book's first chapter, titled "Understanding Time Management," I linked together four features I had
sold as part of my *Market Builder* series: "The Maxims of Time
Management," "Understanding Life Phases," "The Management by
Contract System," and "Self-Generated Motivation." I added two
sidebars, wrote a two-page commentary about how I, personally,
became interested in time management, and then prepared seven
transition paragraphs to aid the reader in getting from one subtopic
to the next. In fewer than four hours, I had organized, written, and
typed an entire chapter. Two more weeks of working like that found
me holding a completed book manuscript.

Step 6: *Sell the Book Manuscript.*
Naturally, your next move is to sell your book. The process is simple. Study the markets until you come up with five book publishers
who have a track record for publishing the kind of book you've
written.

Send one publisher at a time a typed table of contents, a detailed
table of contents containing one paragraph of explanation about each
chapter, one completed chapter, and an SASE.

The cover letter atop all this will be your clincher. Explain in it
that you've sold X number of freelance articles on your book's topic
(this proves not only that you are qualified to write on the subject
but also that there is obvious reader interest in it). Enclose several
published samples from your series and freelance sales.

In my own case, after having written twelve articles on time management and made seventeen reprint sales of those articles, I contacted Bobbs-Merrill Publishing Company with my book proposal for *Staying Ahead of Time*. The company referred it to its business books division, R & R Newkirk, and I was offered a contract. The book was released ten months later.

Step 7: *Sell Excerpts from the Book.*
Once your book appears in print, your next move is to sell excerpts from it. Excerpts put extra cash into your hands as well as help promote your book.

There are several ways to sell excerpts. You or your publisher can send review copies to magazine editors and suggest certain chapters that might be appropriate for their readers. I did this with *Essence* and the editor bought the excerpt rights to Chapter 2 of my book ("The Days of Your Life," March 1982).

You also can write condensations of your chapters, hitting all the high points, and then submit these excerpts for sale to magazines. I did this with *Writer's Digest* ("The Time of Your Life," August 1982) and *Optical Management* ("Time Is on Your Side," March 1983).

Sometimes you can even sell excerpts of your excerpts. I'm serious. After the excerpt from my book appeared in *Writer's Digest*, the editor of *Reader's Digest* paid me fifty dollars to reprint one paragraph of my article in that magazine's "Points to Ponder" column. Similarly, *Leader's Magazine* bought a 750-word excerpt from one of the 2,000-word articles in my series for *Market Builder*.

Step 8: *Develop a Spin-off Topic.*
Once your book is selling and is establishing you as an expert on that topic, begin work on a new series of articles on a closely related topic. This saves you research time, builds on your established reputation, and enables your publisher to promote your books in units or sets.

After publishing *Staying Ahead of Time*, a book on how to make the most of one's time, I wrote *Positive Workaholism*, a book on how to make one's work time more productive. It began as a double series of articles: one series in *Market Builder* and a different series in *ShopTalk*. That book later outsold my previous book four to one. Why? Because my name was already established in the field by the time the new book was released. Success compounds success.

When you look at a giant salami, you realize the only way to eat it all is to cut it into little pieces and to eat one at a time. A book can be written the same way. Slice it into a lot of little articles and you'll be able to handle it like the salami.

And that's no baloney.

SUMMARY

Being prolific and profitable as a freelance writer calls for a knowledge of the writing techniques and marketing procedures that give the greatest return for the least amount of effort. We have reviewed several of those processes in this chapter. Now it's up to you to make use of them.

Action Items

1. If you are currently writing a short story or novel, use the Personality Profile Sheet in this chapter to prepare a dossier on your main character(s).

2. Examine one of your published articles. Using the five Rs found in this chapter (retain, reslant, revise, review, resell), decide how you could do a new version of the article.

3. Review your collection of published articles. Make a list of the articles you have published that have potential to be resold on a cyclical basis.

Suggested Additional Readings

How to Write Best Selling Fiction by Dean Koontz (Cincinnati: Writer's Digest Books, 1980).

How to Write Short Stories That Sell by Louise Boggess (Cincinnati: Writer's Digest Books, 1978).

Writing Without Teachers by Peter Elbow (New York: Oxford University Press, 1975).

5

Mastering the Interview

"Julio?" I repeated.

"Iglesias," confirmed the voice on the other end. "We want you to interview him for the cover story for December's *Saturday Evening Post*.

My teen-age son, hearing only my half of the conversation, paused midbite, put his McNuggets on hold, and flashed me the thumbs-up sign. His head, in the meantime, was bobbing affirmatively like Howdy Doody with a broken mainstring.

Gotcha. Message received. Son-thinks-mom-should-accept-interview-assignment. Mom agrees.

So this is the payback, I thought as I jotted down the travel particulars. "Arrive Nassau at noon," I echoed. "Meet Julio at his villa for private lunch; interview to follow; tour recording studio; back to Miami for the night; fly home the next day." *Ah, yes,* I savored. *This makes up for all the others—the bodybuilder who showed me how to bench press my way to traction* (oh, the pain), *the macrobiotic who convinced me to change my family's diet to brown rice and bancha tea* (near mutiny resulted), *and the psychic who told me a man named David was about to enter and dominate my life* (my husband, Phil, was with me at the time).

I love a good interview. If I didn't, I wouldn't be a writer. The session with the bodybuilder culminated in an as-told-to-Holly-Miller book for him and a new appreciation for weight-lifting athletes for me. The macrobiotic's story fit nicely into the *SatEvePost*'s health and fitness section and taught me to question some of our

American junk food eating habits. The tête-à-tête with the fortune teller became a segment of an article called "City Seers Psych Out the New Year" for *Indianapolis Magazine* and convinced me to leave my husband at home next time.

At the heart of nearly every piece of writing—fiction or nonfiction—is the interview. Skeptical? Check the table of contents in any general-interest magazine for proof. Whether a story is a profile, a "how-to," a news item, an in-depth feature, an opinion piece, or pure fiction, it shares a common element with the others: It's based on an interview. Or interviews. If your goal is to produce an encompassing profile of a person, the interview may span several days and numerous locations. If you're putting together a round-up article in which you're posing a common question to several people, the interviews might be very brief and could even be conducted via telephone or questionnaire. If you're gathering information for a Victorian novel and you need to pick the brain of a local history professor, your interview might take the form of a rambling conversation over coffee. It stands to reason, though, that no matter what your writing specialty is, you need to develop and refine your interviewing skills. How well you perform in an interview setting may determine how often you chalk up freelance sales.

If that's the bad news, the good news is that interviews are fun, and they're the best way I know for an unknown writer to break into print. Profiles, in particular, are the mainstay of every magazine, and the supply of well-written personality pieces simply doesn't equal the demand. Producing a readable interview article is a challenge even for the veteran because the art of interviewing— if we can elevate it to art status—can never be mastered. On several occasions, I've done back-to-back interviews on the same day and felt smugly satisfied with one and totally leveled by the other. I always listen to my tape afterward and critique my performance. The problem, if there is one, is usually obvious and generally rests with me, not the interviewee. I take notice of my shortcoming, learn from it, and vow never to make that particular mistake again.

This is not to say that interviewing is a hit-or-miss exercise. Rules exist, but unfortunately, few writers follow them, and sadly, that's why they remain unpublished authors.

HELLO, YOU DON'T KNOW ME BUT . . .

To ensure a great interview you have to be mentally prepared to seize control of the situation immediately off the blocks. When you're dealing with executives, administrators, celebrities, and professional people, it's essential that you take command from the first moment of contact when you lay down the ground rules. *Your* ground rules. Don't be intimidated. In an interview situation, when you are the interviewer, you are the person in charge. When you call to set up the interview, tell your interviewee exactly how much time you will need. Ask for an hour and never overstay your welcome. At the end of the hour, thank the person for his time and gather together your notes. Only if you're invited to stay should you extend the agreed-upon time limit.

Often, when I make the phone call to request the interview, I explain the kinds of information I'm interested in. This may detract from any surprise element, but it gives the person time to reflect on the topic, recall names, numbers, dates, and anecdotes, and possibly gather any necessary facts, photos, charts, or statistics. I'm not suggesting that you should submit a list of specific questions (absolutely not!), I'm merely saying that if your subject knows what you're interested in, he or she can organize his or her thoughts along those lines. It's a trade-off: The spontaniety is gone, yes, but you'll get better answers. Doctors, business executives, and attorneys traditionally don't like surprises. They're going to be more comfortable if they have some knowledge of the script before they are asked to play a starring role.

BACK TO THE BOOKS

Homework. It can't be stressed enough. The time you spend on your interview before you conduct it often makes the difference between ordinary and extraordinary results. Read everything available on your subject. If he's not well known enough to be listed in *Who's Who* or other library material, call his secretary and ask for his biography. In the case of a person who is not at the top of the management structure, talk to his supervisor or perhaps a coworker. And plan to quote that person. I go on record as being strongly opposed to one-source stories. I like the variety and extra dimension provided by another person. So always get a second opinion. Your subject will be flattered that you cared enough to do a little research and he'll be impressed with your professionalism. If you go into an interview with all the pertinent biographical facts already in your notebook, you don't have to waste valuable time— yours or his. The greatest compliment an interviewee can pay me is to say, "Wow, how'd you know that?"

Your homework also will help you beef up a very short interview into a salable one. It isn't easy to convince a public personality to give an hour or two of his time without any assurance a published article will result. So sometimes a freelancer has to settle for less and make the most of it.

I remember the first time I requested an interview with writer/ humorist Erma Bombeck. She was scheduled to give a lecture at a nearby city and I was determined to wangle a one-on-one with her afterward. My confidence was deflated after dozens of phone calls only yielded a lukewarm invitation to come backstage after the speech and meet her for five minutes. I could have given up in dismay, but instead I went to the library and read everything that was ever written by or about this delightful lady. Then I bought a ticket to her speech. I took my tape recorder along and recorded her prepared remarks. Later, armed with just two or three good questions, I headed backstage . . . along with most of the audience. I tried to get close enough to speak to her but she was surrounded by fans asking for autographs. Finally, I elbowed my way to her side and instead of requesting her to sign my program, I asked my two or three questions. She was wonderful! Graciously she answered the questions and took me aside, plunked herself down on a dusty piano mover and gave me even more time. Still, at best I had fifteen minutes—not much to support a major article for a newspaper. Yet with all my library research and with the information included in her public speech, I was able to sell the article to the local paper and *Writer's Digest* magazine. A couple of months later the Associated Press awarded the story a first-place citation in a writing contest.

Such success stories are common. I have a freelancing pal who was bent on doing an interview with a famous violinist coming to her hometown for a concert. "He's too busy," the musician's agent told her when she requested the interview. Five minutes was the most he could schedule. She did extensive research anyway, and after the violinist's performance she met him backstage to claim her five minutes of his time. He apologized, said he was late to catch his plane, but if she'd like to walk him to his car he'd try to answer a question or two. That's all. They entered the elevator together, the elevator stalled between floors, and my friend, the freelancer, ended up with an hour and a half on tape. Thank goodness she had done her homework!

KNOW WHAT YOU'RE AFTER

What, exactly, do you hope to accomplish with this interview of yours? What's your goal?

Example: I once sold an article on breast cancer to *Today's Christian Woman* magazine. The editor requested it and more or less left it up to me to decide what direction to take. It was a tough assignment because so much has been written on the topic. So what was *my* angle? For one thing, I wanted to inform readers of the latest statistics on how many women have breast cancer, what the survival rate is, new treatments that are available, and where to go for help. I wanted to inspire readers with a few anecdotes about women who are leading happy, productive lives after surgery. I wanted to instruct readers on certain measures that should be taken to increase chances of detecting cancer. I wanted to influence readers by stressing the message that a breast cancer victim should always ask for a second medical opinion, and all women should know how to do a self-examination.

Knowing my purpose and knowing what kind of information I needed to achieve my purpose helped me decide what kinds of questions to ask my interviewees. I planned to talk with doctors about new treatments; I wanted to talk with patients about how they're coping; I hoped to interview spokespersons from the American Cancer Society to get up-to-date statistics; I needed to schedule a phone interview with the Reach for Recovery office to learn about its in-hospital visitation program, and the national YWCA to understand its efforts to build physical and psychological strength in mastectomy patients. And I wanted to interview spouses to learn their role in the cancer experience.

As I mapped out my strategy for gathering information through interviews, it helped to know exactly what my purpose was. Without knowing my direction, I might have run the risk of cranking out a ho-hum formula article, a fill-in-the-blank story that would sound like too many others.

ARE YOU MARRIED?

Not only do I go into an interview with a written list of questions, I make sure they are arranged in a very precise order. I don't want to start out so slowly that my subject becomes bored, but I want to start out slowly enough that he doesn't feel intimidated. I save the toughest questions for last. That way, I've had a chance to build up that all-important rapport, and he'll trust me enough to give a candid answer. Also, if he takes offense and calls a halt to the interview, I have the essential material I need to write a story.

Never ask questions that could have been answered by checking somewhere else—Are you married? Any children? How old are you? And avoid four- and five-part questions. They're confusing. Strive for questions that elicit the person's thoughts, opinions, and feelings rather than yes/no answers or facts you can gather from a biography. Include some open-ended questions as thought provokers. By that, I mean questions such as: What, in the last year, has given you the most pleasure? What do you like and dislike most about yourself? Who are your heroes? What are your favorite books?

Questions like these, rather whimsical in nature, should be used very sparingly and only after your interviewee is relaxed. Always be flexible with questions. Even though you've charted your interview course, be willing to explore new ground if given the chance.

YOUR PLACE OR MINE?

Try to conduct the interview on your interviewee's home turf. His house is best; his office is second best. It helps to see what the person surrounds himself with—the pictures he hangs on the walls, the little personal objects he puts on his desk, the open books by his favorite chair. This isn't always possible and, as interviewers, again we have to be flexible. I've interviewed Roberta Peters in the back of a funeral car and Barbara Mandrell in the back of a bus. But it isn't easy. I particularly dislike trying to conduct an interview in a noisy restaurant where questions have to be alternated with bites of tuna salad. Still, I've talked with Art Buchwald over breakfast, George Burns over lunch, Myrna Loy over high tea, and Colonel Sanders over chicken (mine, not his; he ate a stuffed pepper). Once I interviewed Bob Cummings—remember him?—and he insisted on standing on his head for most of our interview. I don't recommend it.

SHHHHHH!

Plan to spend most of your time listening. I think of a good interviewer as a pushy wallflower. He's aggressive, assertive, and downright pushy when it comes to going after the tough interview. But once he's got it, he settles into a low-key, listener's role.

I learned this the hard way. When I first began doing interviews, I had the irritating habit of stepping on people's answers. I'd ask a question, the person would start to answer it, would hesitate for a minute, and I'd jump in and finish his sentence for him. When I got home and listened to my tape, I heard a lot of Holly Miller quotes, and the sad fact is, no one cares what Holly Miller says about the topic.

So don't be afraid of long pauses during an interview. If you ask a thought-provoking question and the person wants to muse over his answer, let him muse. Chances are, when the answer comes, it will be very quotable. And while you're sitting in the corner being a pushy wallflower, be sure and take notes on your subject's body language. Any interesting expressions? Hand gestures? Does he bite his lip? Fold his arms like Jack Benny? Jab with his finger like Jack Kennedy? Or do his eyebrows jump around like a couple of caterpillars on a trampoline? Such observations add color to your story.

LIMIT YOUR VISION

Don't try to find out everything about your subject. Focus on one or two areas. Remember, a profile is not a biography. You are not simply writing about a person. You're writing about some trait, talent or circumstance that makes him noteworthy and interesting. You don't have to trace his childhood, include all his academic degrees and accomplishments, and his philosophy toward life, politics, and religion, and then close with the stock sentence, "He is married to the former Mary Smith and they have two children."

If you must recount his early childhood, think in terms of a separate sidebar—related to the main story, but not a part of it. Some major stories have several sidebars, placed close to the central story but all with separate headlines. *Example:* When I did an article on military schools and how they're coming back into vogue, I included a sidebar of quotes from several famous people who were graduated from military institutions. When I wrote a story about Disney World, I added a sidebar on what it costs a family of four to spend a week in the Magic Kingdom.

FOR POSTERITY (AND ACCURACY)

Use a tape recorder. Ask permission by explaining that the interview will be quicker and more accurate. I always say that I'm left-handed—which I am—and I have terrible penmanship—which I do—and I would appreciate his O.K. on my using a recorder. I have a fleet of the little machines, by the way, and my latest acquisition is a tiny microrecorder, excellent for when you have to conduct an interview while walking. It's tiny, fits into the palm of my hand, is very lightweight, and is voice activated.

Recorders enable you to sit back, make eye contact, and enjoy the interview without being hunched over a pad making chicken scratches with a pen that invariably runs dry. You'll also have much more material to recycle into second, third, and fourth articles.

HURRY UP

Don't wait too long to write your article. It's amazing how all the personal touches of your interview will fade if you procrastinate. Write it while you still feel the electricity of the encounter.

WHO, ME?

A pet peeve of mine! When it comes to putting your interview on paper, leave yourself out of it. In other words, fight the temptation to include yourself in the story. No first-person interviews, please.

An editor once reminded me that suicide notes are always written in the first person, and droning on about your role in an interview can be journalistic suicide. Forget it, and play it straight.

SUMMARY

An interview gives you the opportunity to find out everything you ever wanted to know about a person but didn't have an excuse to ask. Play devil's advocate; get inside his brain; prod it; challenge it; watch it work. The interview process should be painless and professional, even fun—for both of you. Plot your questions carefully, ask them kindly, and always leave the door open for a return visit or a follow-up phone call.

Action Items

1. Choose someone you would like to interview. He might be famous, infamous, living, or dead. How would you go about doing your homework before your appointment?

2. List ten thought-provoking questions, arranged in logical order, that you would ask during the course of your interview.

Suggested Additional Readings

Talking Woman by Shana Alexander (New York: Delacorte Press, 1976).

How to Talk with Practically Anybody about Practically Anything by Barbara Walters (Garden City, N.Y.: Doubleday and Co., Inc., 1970).

6

Earning Bucks by Bucking the Trends

Gypsy Rose Lee used to say, "To succeed in show business, ya gotta have a gimmick." To some extent that's also true of publishing. It is often the unusual topic or writing format that will grab the attention of an editor and, consequently, the reading public.

In this chapter we are going to examine ways in which you can interview expert sources (thus building on the skills you learned in the previous chapter) and then use those interviews to develop unique and unusual writing topics.

DISCOVERING THE UNUSUAL

In publishing, trying to jump on the popular topic bandwagon can often leave writers with sore backsides if their timing isn't perfect. The bandwagon frequently seems to move ahead too quickly.

Traditional wisdom holds that in order to be successful at marketing freelance writing, one must jump on the bandwagon (whatever people are excited about) and start writing about it. And sometimes that works . . . that is, if the bandwagon hangs around long enough for the writer to get something in print about it.

But my nontraditional experience has shown me that jumping off the bandwagon can often prove to be more successful. For one thing, there's virtually no competition when you're alone.

Frequently, when public opinion is leaning strongly one way, I purposely write something that supports the minority view. And without fail (if my writing has been done well), I meet with amazing success.

A CASE IN POINT

In the late 1970s and early 1980s, the popular press was filled with articles and books that denounced workaholism. The workaholic was portrayed as a neurotic, masochistic, self-slave-driver who was chained to his job and who desperately needed psychiatric counseling. Everyone from respected physicians to pop psychologists on the radio was taking shots at the workaholic.

To me, these people were all wet. I had been a card-carrying workaholic since I was twelve and I knew it to be a great way of life. And I said so in print.

In 1983, my book *Positive Workaholism* was released by the R & R Newkirk Publishing Company. It carried the subtitle, "Making the Most of Your Potential." The book punched holes in the arguments of the so-called experts who had denounced workaholism as something negative. The book went on to teach people how to *become* workaholics by increasing their energy levels, using their time more effectively, and developing their mental strength to its capacity.

The book was iconoclastic, singular in its view, and aggressively belligerent in its rebuttal of the then-popular negative view of workaholism. And the book was one other thing: incredibly successful.

It took off like a shot. In June 1983, *Success* magazine devoted an entire page to the book, giving it its highest praise. *Christian Business Life Digest* devoted two full pages to a review of the book and rated it four stars. United Press International did a wire story about my writing career and how I had conceived the "positive workaholic" theory.

Excerpts from the book were purchased by seventeen magazines. It became R & R Newkirk's top-selling book for 1983. In 1984, Success Motivation, Inc., of Waco, Texas, purchased the audio rights to the book and made a successful cassette tape series out of it. I was in demand for appearances on radio and TV talk shows from Fort Wayne to Seattle.

As it turned out, there were thousands of closet workaholics who related perfectly to what my book had said. They not only bought copies for themselves, they bought second and third copies to give to friends, colleagues, and spouses.

And the circumstance regarding that book was no freak one-time incident. About that same time, I wrote a long magazine article titled, "Why I Fought in Vietnam and Why I'd Do It Again." The article was based on my personal experience as a U.S. Army sergeant in South Vietnam in 1971. It argued that the United States had made a good decision to intervene in Southeast Asia and that there were many positive results that had come out of the Vietnam War. Obviously this was not the popular opinion of the press media in America at that time.

The article was published in *The Baptist Bulletin* (May 1984) and the positive response it received caught even me off guard. Letters of praise and thanks came to me from veterans' associations, editors, readers, clergymen, and writer friends of mine. Two Christian book publishers contacted me and asked for other samples of my work. One of those publishers later signed me to five major book contracts. All that, simply because I was willing to verbalize the views of a silent, but unified, minority segment of society.

GOING AGAINST THE GRAIN

A recent best-seller by Terry Cole-Whittaker titled *How to Have More in a Have-Not World* (Rawson Associates, 1983) shows that other writers have discovered the marketability of the odd-book-out theory.

Cole-Whittaker took a look at lines in the Bible such as, "The meek shall inherit the earth" and "The love of money is the root of all evil" and decided they shouldn't be taken literally. Her book proclaims that God actually wants people to be wealthy, powerful, and prestigious. I am at complete odds with this woman's theology, but the fact that her book sold more than 90,000 copies does prove that you can get rich by writing about nontraditional views on things.

When you consider it, there has been an element of tradition-bucking in many of the nonfiction best-sellers of this decade. The underlying message of *The One-Minute Manager* was that, no, you don't have to attend college for six years to earn an MBA in order to be an effective manager; all you really need to do is learn the three basic concepts in that book. And, whereas I personally feel that that book was oversimplified, I can't deny its incredible success.

So then, since it's obvious that swimming against the popular literary tide can be profitable, the next step is to learn how to do it.

Step 1: *Determine the Current Popular Opinions.*
Scrutinize the newspapers and magazines that come into your house. Clip any articles that seem to present a slanted or biased approach to any topic. Start a folder. Review it frequently. Group collections of articles that seem to have the same theme.

Step 2: *Make a List of Counterpoint Views.*
On a piece of paper, make two columns. On the left side, list the themes of the various article collections you have gathered from your folder. On the right side, list the opposite viewpoints.

Don't worry at this stage about whether or not you agree with the counterpoint views; just list them. For example, in the left column you may have an entry that reads, "Nuclear waste dumps cause community panic, lower real estate values, and potential health hazards." Across from that, in the right column, you would write, "Nuclear waste dumps provide a national service and provide work opportunities to on-site residents."

To expand this list, you can check the best-seller lists of the *New York Times Review of Books* and *Publishers Weekly* and make a list of all the books that focus on the same topic from the same viewpoint. You then can determine what the opposite opinion would be. For example, in 1978, when gold rose to $830 an ounce, the best-seller lists were burdened with pro-gold books written by Harry Browne, Howard Ruff, Geoffry Abert, Adam Smith, and Douglas R. Casey. That same year, a friend of mine wrote a well-researched freelance article titled, "Why Gold Will Crash to $250 an Ounce by 1985." The article sold its first time out (to an investments magazine, which paid $400 for it).

Step 3: *Examine the List for the Most Promising Topics.*
After coming up with a list of ten or twelve counterpoint topics, you must focus on the best opportunities you will have for developing credible articles. You can determine this by answering four questions in regard to each topic:

1. Do I have a strong enough personal opinion about this topic to motivate me to present it with my best journalistic talents?
2. Can I find experts on this subject who will allow themselves to be quoted as endorsing an unpopular view? (More on this will be discussed later in this chapter.)
3. Am I certain that no other author has already written an article or book that presents this counterpoint view?
4. Can I think of at least five freelance markets that might at least entertain the idea of publishing such an alternative opinion on this topic?

Finding one or two topics from your list that will meet the criteria of all four questions won't be easy. However, those topics that do survive the screening will have strong potential for marketing.

Step 4: *Query Editors and Prepare the Submission.*
Writing a concise and highly focused query letter will help you clarify and pinpoint your approach to the counterpoint topic. Mail the query as soon as it's ready, but keep a copy to use as your article writing guide.

In preparing your article, use an offensive rather than defensive writing style. Your lead should be an opening salvo that immediately informs the reader that you mean to take issue with a popularly held view. This lead should be followed by a statement from a credible source so that the reader will be forced to at least give your idea the temporary benefit of the doubt. Additional data (statistics, case histories, references) to further support your claims are also needed early in the article so that the reader will know you are not writing an editorial but are, in fact, presenting a well-researched article.

It's important to bring in a "human factor," too. The reader will be wondering what impact this whole concept of yours can have on him or her. You must respond to that by giving a dramatic statement or an anecdote or a projection that the reader will be able to identify with. (See sidebar for a sample article lead.)

The balance of the article will have three objectives: to summarize differing opinions and to respond to them; to help the reader

---

Phases of a Counterpoint Article's Lead

Why Mandatory Death Penalties Are Needed Nationally

By Fred Freelancer

People who have been against the death penalty as a deterrent to crime may soon need to reserve their opinions.

OPENING SALVO

"Even though I hate to admit it," says liberal attorney Kim Davis of the Elkins, Davis and McCormick law firm of Washington, "the fact is, states with the death penalty have substantially lower crime rates than those without it. Those sorts of results are causing more and more state legislatures to reconsider lifting the ban on state executions."

CREDIBLE SOURCE

Recent statistics from the International Deputies Association show that hardened criminals who are pardoned from execution and subsequently released from prison return to a life of crime in 37 percent of the cases.

ADDITIONAL SUPPORT DATA

Law enforcement officials aren't impressed by statistical reports, however.

"Statistics? You want statistics?" says Federal Marshal Dave Ramey of Crosscreek, New Mexico. "Well, here's one for you. Half the murderers released from prison go out and kill again. But one hundred percent of the ones who go to the chair never commit another murder. Those are the only statistics a lawman can rely on."

HUMAN FACTOR

see the full scope of the topic; and to present enough facts, quotes, and examples to win the reader over to the author's viewpoint. Of course, that will require adequate research on your part.

Whereas editors are not open to ludicrous counterpoint topic articles, such as "Cancer Can Improve Your Health" or "Street Gangs Can Control the Population Boom," they nevertheless are open to sharing minority views with their readers. Their criteria for accepting such articles are strict: thorough research; credible sources; excellent writing.

Meet those requirements and you'll earn yourself an audience. Keep in mind that despite the fact that the current runs against it, a determined salmon can still make it upstream. So can you.

USING EXPERT SOURCES

We noted earlier that using quotations from experts gives your article more credibility.

A large stock brokerage firm once had an advertising slogan that stated, "When E. F. Hutton talks, people listen." The implied message was that whenever an expert offers an opinion on something, people pay attention.

It's not a new concept. In 50 B.C. the Roman poet Virgil wrote, "Believe a person who has proved it himself. Believe an expert."

People *do* believe experts. Knowing this, freelance writers can double or triple their chances of selling articles by making a point to quote experts. Let's face it: Whose opinion on Toyota automobiles carries more weight with you: your neighbor who owns a Toyota or a mechanic who has worked on nine hundred Toyotas? The mechanic, of course. Get the point?

Whether you are aware of it or not, you are already in the habit of citing expert sources all the time. In your conversations, you are frequently apt to say things like, "I've got this friend in real estate who tells me . . ." or "As my old grandfather used to say . . ." By bringing in the expertise of an outside person, you give your story more believability and authenticity. The same thing applies to article writing.

Besides authenticity, however, quotes from experts give your article more depth, a greater variety of opinions, and a break from the monotony of just presenting *your* words. If put into a sidebar, they can even provide a format variation for your article.

Finding experts on given topics is not difficult. Very few experts are famous. Any person with appropriate credentials (your pastor, your family physician, your college professors) can serve as an expert source.

You can give your article national appeal by citing sources outside your local sphere. There are several ways to go about this:

1. *Tape Record Radio and TV Interviews.*
You may quote from someone else's interview as long as you don't seriously diminish the value of the original program by "borrowing" too heavily. Remember to cite your reference (interviewer, interviewee, show, station or network, and date).

2. *Quote from Original Articles and Books Written by Experts.*
This is perfectly legal, especially if you quote fewer than 250 words. For courtesy's sake, most writers will send a letter to the publisher seeking permission to quote from a book. It seldom, if ever, is denied. (Most writers and publishers are grateful for the publicity.)

3. *Read Specialty Periodicals and Organizational Publications, and Quote the Publications Themselves.*
There's nothing wrong with saying, "A Harris Poll cited in *Newsweek* on July 19 showed that . . ." or "According to an editorial in *Christianity Today* in May of this year . . ."

4. *Conduct Mail Interviews with Experts.*
Send a form letter to eight or ten experts on the topic you plan to write about. With the letter, attach a page of questions (from five to fifteen) and enclose an SASE. Usually only three out of ten will take the time to respond, but three experts are all you need.

5. *Call the Public Relations or Publicity Directors of Universities, Businesses, and Organizations.*
Ask for an interview appointment with someone who is an expert on your topic or interest. Hospitals, fraternal organizations, and political parties also have helpful P.R. personnel who can arrange

for you to interview key people. Tell them you want to talk to someone with a substantial track record in that area of interest and who is currently "on the cutting edge" in knowledge, research, and production.

6. Conduct Phone Interviews.

The phone interview is probably the best of these six techniques. (Long distance phone calls related to article research are as tax deductible as expenses for maintenance of your word processor or costs for mailing manuscripts.)

A phone interview gives your hometown articles national scope. Begin by going to the *Reader's Guide to Periodical Literature* in the reference section of your local library. Look up articles written during the past five years about your topic. Locate copies of these articles, read them, and make a note of the authors and the experts cited in the articles. Call their hometowns by area code plus 555-1212 and ask the information operator for their telephone numbers.

When you phone the experts, explain what your topic is, which publication you plan to market the article to, and why you feel he or she would make a good resource person. Ask when it would be convenient for you to call back to talk for thirty minutes with the person. Set up a specific appointment.

In the interim, read all you can by and about the expert you will be interviewing. Prepare a long list of questions. Since your article will probably cite at least three experts, you may want different experts to focus on different questions on your list.

When you make your follow-up call, remember to inform the expert that you are taping the interview. Also, ask the person to send a photo of himself or herself to you. As you talk, try to get the expert's thoughts, opinions, feelings, and predictions about the topic rather than just statistics. The facts you do need to get, however, should be checked for accuracy at the end of the interview (spelling of names and places, dates, etc.). Keep a notepad in front of you to supplement the tape recorder and to note any hesitancies, reactions, drawls, or other attention-arresting factors.

When you transcribe your tapes for your article, feel free to exercise poetic license in correcting a person's grammar and in condensing the person's sentences, so long as the meaning stays the same. For example, the tape recorder may have, "Let's see, I, uh, came out here around—oh, what was it?—around 1983 . . . in June, now that I think of it." When that quote appears in your article it will read, "I came here in June of 1983."

To help the reader "see" the expert, you may wish to add a few descriptive or scene-setting words, such as, "Dr. Graham paused, cleared his throat, then replied, 'Of course, back then we had no idea that cyclamates could cause cancer.'"

In order to keep your source people loyal to you, it pays to take the time to send each one a copy of your article that mentions them after it appears in print. (This is the *only pay* any expert should expect to receive for time and services.)

There's something in all of us that makes us want to get something for nothing, including free advice from experts. If your articles can offer such free advice, *you* will become an *expert* on manuscript sales.

THE "AS TOLD TO" FEATURE

Frequently, as you are interviewing various experts, you will discover a person who has developed a concept worthy of being published as an article or book. You can take advantage of the opportunity of working with this person: Let the expert tell you about his or her research and then publish it as an "as told to" article.

Many people have had personal experiences, business experiences, cultural and social and religious experiences that are the makings of fascinating articles or books. Their only problem—and it's a substantial one—is that they don't have the professional writing skills needed to record and market their experiences.

That's where we come in. There's nothing to prevent these people from telling us their stories and allowing us to write them. This is done all the time. Such books and articles carry "as told to" bylines and are produced as a team effort.

I've done several "as told to" articles over the years. The first time it happened, I was approached by a child psychologist at a leading midwestern university, who asked me to take his research and convert it into a general interest article. Another time, a magazine editor gave me three cassette tapes in which a successful insurance agent explained his sales techniques; my job was to convert the taped talk into an article. Yet another time, I spent half an hour on the phone with a fashion designer who explained to me about his new fall line; using my notes of that conversation, I wrote an "as told to" feature.

Generally there are four instances in which the "as told to" story is employed:

1. A famous person, such as a professor or physician or scientist, needs assistance in explaining his or her knowledge in layman's language.
2. A famous person, such as a politician, actor, or musician, wants help in publicizing his or her career by writing an autobiography.
3. A wealthy or successful person wishes to explain the secrets of his or her success but does not have the time or writing skill to do a book.
4. An unknown person goes through an incredible experience, such as giving birth to sextuplets or being awarded the Congressional Medal of Honor or winning the Betty Crocker Bake-Off, and an editor assigns a professional writer to help that person tell his or her story to the world.

If you are interested in writing "as told to" articles, there are several ways to line up assignments. One way is by carefully reading your local newspapers and discovering people who are experts in certain areas and then contacting them with the idea of working together on a book or article. For example, if you happen to read a notice of a retirement party for an ex-conductor of a railroad, he could be a good source for travelogues, nostalgia pieces, adventure narratives, or historical documentaries.

You might also want to place small ads in professional journals:

AVAILABLE: Freelance writer specializing in "as told to" articles for trade/technical/professional publications. References available. Rates negotiable. Contact John Q. Writer, Box 119, % this magazine.

You can also send letters to publishers, editors, and literary

agents announcing your availability, stating your rates, and presenting your credentials. It won't take long for job offers to start
coming your way.

ESTABLISHING RATES

You'll need an answer for the first time someone calls you up and
says, "I want to write a book about our family tree. How much will
you charge to help me?" or "I have tape-recorded fifteen of my best
sermons and I was wondering what your rates would be to develop
them into a book manuscript."

I usually judge my rate on the circumstances related to the assignment. If the person I'm working with stands to benefit greatly
from the publication of the proposed article, I insist on keeping the
royalty check for myself. For example, if professors don't get published, they don't get tenure (the "publish or perish" syndrome).
So if my article based on some professor's research lands him a
better office, a new title, and a $2,000-per-year raise, the least he
can do is let me keep the check from the magazine.

If I'm commissioned by an editor to help someone write his or
her personal experience story, I estimate how long the assignment
will take me and I bill the editor at an hourly rate.

If I approach someone, such as a doctor or busy industrialist, and
ask him or her to interrupt his or her professional schedule in order
to help me write a magazine article, I share both the byline and
the royalty check equally with that person.

FOLLOWING A FORMAT

When writing the "as told to" feature, you must pretend that you
are controlling the other person's hand and that he or she is actually
doing the writing. At times it will be strange. If you are a woman
freelance writer preparing a man's article, it will seem odd for you
to write something in the first person such as, "I love to hug and
kiss my wife and smell her sweet perfume." But remember, although you are the writer, *it's not your story.* It has only been told
to you and you are repeating it as you have heard it.

Your writing should be filled with facts and anecdotes. Be sure to double-check all facts—spelling of names, exact dates, numbers, towns, quotes. Do not trust the memory of your collaborator. Use old newspapers, an almanac, company archives, and other references to provide verified statistics and data for your article.

Probe your collaborator for his or her recollections, feelings, opinions, and ideas. Try to discover the humor, pathos, irony, and optimism of every story.

Keep your "as told to" narrative lively. Use short sentences. Go easy on adjectives and adverbs, and rely more on strong verbs and nouns. Keep the element of human drama out front.

Prior to submitting the article for publication, have your source person read and approve the manuscript. Have him or her sign a release for the story. Keep the release on file.

Once the article appears in print, you will receive several calls from potential new source people. But don't be surprised if former

---

Sample Collaborator Release Form

I have carefully read the article _____(title)_____
by _____(freelancer's name)_____ and I approve its use for publication purposes. I understand that my name may also appear on the article as an author. I further give my permission for photographs of myself and other subjects/items/settings related to the article to be used for publication. I hereby release the author from any liability for editing or alteration of the article that may be done by editors or publishers of the periodical(s) planning to print this article.

Date _____   _____

                                    (signature)

                                    _____

                                    (address)

Witness _____   _____

---

co-byliners call you again. Once people get byline fever, they find it hard to shake.

Action Items

1. Pull together a stack of current magazines and newspapers. Using the four-step procedure explained in this chapter, prepare a list of counterpoint topics related to contemporary news events or topics. Focus on one of these topics and send out a query to an editor to see if you can get the authorization needed to pursue this topic.

2. Make a list of people you know who are experts in their fields. Consider your relatives, neighbors, colleagues at work, friends at church, old school chums, and business associates. Review the list and decide which two or three people would be the best candidates for an "as told to" feature about their research or careers. Call or write to them and set up an interview appointment.

3. If you are keenly interested in one or two particular counterpoint topics, begin now to build files on these subjects. Save articles and newspaper clippings that relate to these subjects. If someone is interviewed on radio or TV who is an expert on those subjects, take notes of the interview and keep them in your file.

Suggested Additional Readings

Become Famous, Then Rich by Dennis E. Hensley (Chicago: R & R Newkirk Co., 1983).

The Craft of Interviewing by John Brady (Cincinnati: Writer's Digest Books, 1979).

Stalking the Feature Story by William Ruehlmann (Cincinnati: Writer's Digest Books, 1974).

Writing for Profit by Dennis E. Hensley (Nashville: Thomas Nelson Co., 1985).

7

Satisfying the Reader

As an author, your goal is to write in so simple a manner, no one can misunderstand your message. Naturally, in order to sustain interest, this must be done with style. But simplicity of message will always remain your prime objective.

People read magazine articles expecting to take away something from them. It's this "take away" that makes any article valuable.

If an article has promised to show how to make a home more secure from burglaries, and the reader finishes the article and knows six ways to improve his home security, that "take away" has justified the reader's time. The reader feels satisfied.

Reader satisfaction, then, is earned in two ways: first, by writing in a clear and understandable style; and second, by making the article's content of value to the reader. Usually, if a writer does adequate research, his articles will have enough substance to provide readers with a satisfying "take away."

However, not all magazine articles have a writing style that makes a reader feel, "Yes, this makes sense and, sure, I can see where the writer is going with this line of thought."

To achieve that, everything about your article or story must flow so normally and appear so logical the reader will never realize he is being led along a predetermined line of thought. Everything should seem natural. Everything should blend: The title should be appropriate for what is actually covered in the article or story; the introduction should set a tone that will be carried throughout the piece; and the facts presented should all be pertinent to the topic being discussed. All this can best be accomplished by writing in logical patterns that readers quickly recognize and feel comfortable following. (*Note:* See Chapter 4's section on "Writing Articles Impromptu" for other writing patterns involving organizing formats.)

KNOWING THE PATTERNS

People tend to think and evaluate things according to patterned responses. Although these responses are personal in the sense that each person possesses a unique mind, they are also universal in that we all have retained similar language development patterns.

If an author can learn the patterns by which human logic and human thought are translated into language, that author will have the key to the formula for successful article writing. In short, he will know how to satisfy the reader.

Let's review the six most common response patterns, with an example of how each might be employed in writing an article.

Pattern 1: *Present a Problem and the Reader Will Expect a Solution.*

Example:

In 1936, Nick Benton's grandfather, Marshall Benton, leased eighteen acres of the Benton farm to a church for fifty years at one dollar per year. The church created a cemetery on the tract. The lease is now up and Nick wants the bodies removed. He plans to farm that land. The church wants things left as they are.

The Davis County Coroner's Office has suggested a compromise: Why not exhume the coffins and put them into a mausoleum that can be built near the church? The concerned parties plan to meet on Saturday to review this option.

Notice how reader interest was piqued by presenting the problem of what to do with a graveyard filled with bodies that have to be moved. In this example, the reader is offered a possible solution when it is suggested that the bodies could be exhumed and put into a mausoleum. From a straight news reporting perspective, that *satisfies* the reader by providing a logical projection of what will most likely happen.

But that explanation could have been delayed until the end of the article if the author's purpose had been to discuss how dignity can be guaranteed for humans after death. In the end, the reader would have been just as *satisfied,* but his "take away" would have been a greater understanding of the moral and legal issues related to disturbing the dead.

Pattern 2: *Pose a Question and the Reader Will Anticipate a Forthcoming Answer.*

Example:

Have you ever wondered how kids from wonderful homes can sometimes wind up as drug addicts? Well, after nine years of interviewing many such young people, Dr. Louise Markham of the Strosen Clinic of Toledo believes she knows why. According to Dr. Markham . . .

Here we see that the reader has been challenged to solve a mystery (why good kids get hooked on drugs). Questions are small mysteries, and we all want to know whodunnit. It's human nature to want to answer a riddle, break a code, provide a correct answer. When a question is posed in an article, the reader can only discover the answer by reading the entire article. So the reader reads on.

This puts the author in control. If the author wishes to use a journalistic format, he can move right into the answer (as in our example). If he wants to write a short story, he may want to start unfolding the tale of Mary Smith, whose circumstances in the story explain how her wealthy parents had no time for her so she turned to drugs for solace. The author may even wish to write a magazine article that begins by presenting the same question but then proceeds to offer six different responses from respected authorities in counseling and psychiatry.

The format opportunities are endless and each can be successful, so long as the author *satisfies* the reader by sooner or later providing the answer to the question that had been posed.

Pattern 3: *Summarize the Past and the Reader Will Expect It Somehow to Apply to the Present.*

Example:

A billion hours ago was the emergence of life on earth. A billion minutes ago was the birth of Christ. A billion seconds ago was the Japanese attack on Pearl Harbor. A billion dollars ago was yesterday in Congress.

This pattern is obvious in its approach. Whenever you made a mistake when you were young, your mother or dad would say, "Now, when I was a kid . . ." The story that was then told always had a bearing on the current situation. It's a common technique used to provide perspective on a situation. It works. Just make sure the reader sees the parallel you are drawing between then and now.

Pattern 4: *Tell of an Action and the Reader Will Want You to Explain the Reaction.*

Example:

Studying U.S.–Soviet relations last year was like watching a chess game. When the U.S. put new missiles in West Germany, the Russians put new bombers in Cuba. When the U.S. sent aircraft carriers to the Mediterranean Sea, the Russians converged a pack of submarines forty miles off the coast of Maryland.

And now, this month, the U.S. has sent CIA advisors into the Communist provinces of Nicaragua, and Washington is biting its nails waiting to see what Moscow will come up with as a counter ploy.

This example shows that point and counterpoint threats and bargains are integral parts of our lives. A child will say, "Don't come into my yard or I'll tell my mother." An adult will say, "Either we get fifty cents more an hour or we go on strike."

Readers identify quickly with action–reaction circumstances. For the fiction writer, this means that if, for example, one character sets fire to another character's house in chapter three, the reader will expect some sort of retaliation a few chapters later. When such a scene takes place, the reader is *satisfied* that a logical response cycle has been completed.

For the article writer, the technique is best used when a writer wants to explain (or justify) why something transpired as it did. For instance, by explaining John Hinckley, Jr.'s traumatic childhood, an author can help readers understand why the young man sought attention by shooting President Reagan. Deciding whether what he did was right or wrong is not the duty of the author, only the job of explaining *how* it came about. That is all that is needed to satisfy the reader.

Pattern 5: *Denounce Something as Wrong and the Reader Will Expect You to Proclaim What is Right.*

Example:

Our system of financing the government is illogical and counterproductive. The IRS is too powerful, taxes are too high, and the paperwork is too burdensome. Only one thing can purge us of this mess: the "flat tax" assessment. This innovative approach is based on . . .

The function of lectures, editorials, debates, and even letters to the editor is to sway people to the presenter's way of thinking; to view a matter with similar appreciation. Before someone can be made to accept a new point of view, he first must be convinced that his old point of view is not in his best interest. He must be convinced to re-view his stance.

This is best accomplished by mentioning important facts and ideas the reader may not have previously considered. If you can present enough facts to indicate that the reader's current viewpoint may be flawed, the reader will want to discover your ideas for correcting the problems.

Pattern 6: *Offer a General Overview of Something, and the Reader Will Assume You Will Eventually Move to Discussing Its Specific Aspects.*

Example:

Space exploration has cost the U.S. taxpayers more than $63 billion since 1958. NASA has helped man walk in space, orbit the earth, even drive a Land Rover on the moon. It's been a great show. But has it been worth that much money?

At least one American feels it has been. Says Senator Delbert Jones of Wyoming, "Why, just inventing Teflon coating, transistorized electronics, and freeze-dried foods has more than justified the expenses. The moon walk was nothing. The side benefits we've gained from the space program, that's what's made the investment so worthwhile."

This writing pattern makes use of the fact that the human mind can only be temporarily impressed by monumental events. For a lasting impact, events must be reduced to memorable quantities. For instance, you can be greatly impressed by the enormity of the Chicago Field Museum; but having visited it, what you will recall will be small, individual exhibits. Your mind will have reduced an overwhelming experience to a series of retainable, specific memories, each with some particular appeal to you. The experience was stunning, but the *satisfaction* came from the small units you could directly relate to.

Knowing this, a writer can grab a reader's attention with an incredible opening statement, but then provide a "take away" by focusing on one important part of the overall circumstance. By way of example, one could report that 19 million people starved to death in Africa last year (a startling and tragic general summary of a circumstance); then the writer could tell the personal account of Bin Jumul, an Ethiopian who buried all five of his children during a journey to find food for his family. This *satisfies* the reader that the writer had not overstated his report.

SUPPORT FROM WRITING TECHNIQUES

By understanding and using these six standard response patterns, you can select the most appropriate writing format to use and you can judge in advance what your reader's expectations will be. They are workable systems.

Newer writers should adhere to a standardized approach to article writing, which allows full use of the response patterns. Here are some guidelines:

- Remember to establish the context of whatever is being discussed in each section of your article. This can be done by using subtitles, topic sentences, or statements of the problem.
- Provide point-blank answers to the who, what, when, where, why, how, and how much questions that most readers will have about your topic. Provide adequate details and explanations on all matters.
- Correlate all of your data and show how your topic specifically relates to the reader as information or entertainment. Make sure all transitions are smooth. Include copy that either moves the action forward or provides essential information.
- End your article by offering a summary of your subject or by making a prediction of how your subject will have an impact on the future.

To hold your reader's interest and to maintain your reins upon his thoughts, you must present no ramblings, tangential ideas, or superfluous thoughts. Readers don't like tricks; they want straight information presented in an easy-to-follow format. By presenting your material according to the standard reader response patterns, you'll always have satisfied readers.

Action Items

1. Pull out one of your manuscripts that has been rejected several times by editors. Using the reader response patterns you learned in this chapter, rewrite your manuscript and send it out again.

2. Memorize all six reader response patterns. Go to your ideas file and pull out some notes for a pending project. Decide which writing pattern would best apply to it. Write the article.

3. Take a current magazine and read several of the articles. Using different colored felt-tip pens, underline the key passages and identify which response patterns the author is using for the article.

Suggested Additional Readings

The Elements of Style by William Strunk, Jr., and E. B. White (New York: Macmillan, 1972).

On Writing Well by William Zinsser (New York: Harper & Row, 1976).

Writing to Sell by Scott Meredith (New York: Harper & Row, 1974).

8
Tapping
Uncommon Markets

Bread. Dallas Christian Family. To Dragma. Carpet Retailing. KMC TV Program Guide. Right Down the Road. The Kappa Alpha Theta. Charisma.

Chances are, the publications listed above aren't currently strewn across your coffee table or waiting their turn in the "must read" stack on your nightstand. Never heard of them, you say? Neither had I; at least not until I changed my sales strategy, began tapping the uncommon markets, and started banking lucrative returns for my efforts.

One of the differences between competitive and novice freelancers is that the veteran thinks small and gets big results while the newcomer dreams big and gets no results. Let me explain.

Of the more than ten thousand periodicals now being published in the United States, only six hundred are classified as general interest magazines. Into this category fall the "giants" recognized by everyone: *Reader's Digest* with its 17.8 million subscribers, *TV Guide, National Geographic, Newsweek, Better Homes and Gardens,* and other commonly known magazines. These are the markets many beginning freelancers consider as prime targets for their first query letters and manuscripts. Admittedly, payments from these magazines are great, but the competition is incredible. And the backlog. I know this firsthand, since I've sold to the top two— *Reader's Digest* and *TV Guide*—and anxiously waited more than a year to see my words in print.

The competitive writer has the foresight to consider, but the vision to look beyond, the giants. If ten thousand magazines are published in the United States and only six hundred are general interest publications, what about the others? What about the thirteen hundred religious/inspirational periodicals . . . the seven hundred agricultural publications . . . the twenty-five-hundred-plus business and trade journals? What about specialty publications like *Bread* (a monthly geared to junior and senior high schoolers in the Church of the Nazarene)? And *Carpet Retailing* (a quarterly published by Monsanto for carpet retailers)? And *To Dragma* (the official magazine for members of Alpha Omicron Pi international sorority)? All of these maintain small staffs, depend on freelance submissions, and pay decent rates.

Perhaps most important for the beginning freelancer, each of these magazines accords its contributors sizable bylines in 12-point type—a "perk" every novice covets. The byline becomes a marketing tool in itself when copies of the published article are attached to queries and mailed to publications with even larger circulations. Suddenly the beginner is elevated to the rank of "published author," with clippings to prove it.

BUT I'M NOT A BAPTIST

Stock advice given by every English composition teacher to her students is this: "Write about familiar topics." But the competitive writer knows this isn't always possible. Or practical. If only Kiwanians wrote for *Kiwanis Magazine* or only senior citizens wrote for *Modern Maturity* or only handicapped persons wrote for *Disabled USA,* many interesting topics, sensitive writing styles, and probing interviews would never be included in the pages of these publications. But they are. Uncommon magazines often serve nontraditional audiences; and the author need not feel he or she has to belong to that audience in order to write for it.

Jan Moore, a successful midwestern freelancer, worked her way through graduate school by selling variations on the same theme to a number of Christian denominational magazines. The pay per piece wasn't generous—sometimes only pennies a word—but when the sales were multiplied four or five times, the bottom line was enough to underwrite her college expenses. Editors didn't mind her strategy since they knew their readerships didn't overlap.

Baptists don't read Presbyterian publications; Methodists don't subscribe to Catholic journals; Lutherans never see Episcopalian tabloids. What all church members have in common, however, is an interest in people, events, and issues. For instance, Jan's interview with Carl Erskine, legendary Brooklyn Dodger pitcher and father of a severely handicapped child, was sought-after copy whose merit was recognized by several inspirational magazine editors. Similar articles that investigate hot topics, offer insights into colorful personalities, or shed light on pertinent issues will be welcome additions to any church publication, regardless of denomination. The competitive writer recognizes this, knows the editorial bent of each market, and thus tailors the product to satisfy the reader's curiosity and the editor's guidelines.

"Simultaneous submissions are fine," says Rich Willowby, managing editor of *Vital Christianity*. "But I don't like these 'one-size-fits-all' articles. Very few articles work for a variety of publications without some alterations. I get about three thousand unsolicited manuscripts a year and two thirds of them aren't worth looking at."

Willowby includes among his pet peeves articles that are accompanied by cover notes saying, "The Lord told me to write this."

Says Willowby, "I'm tempted to reply, 'I wonder why He didn't tell me it was coming, then?' "

Also on the *verboten* list is writing that is overspiritualized and laden with ethereal phrases like "glory to God," "hallelujah," and "sanctification." Says Willowby, "Some novice writers can write ten pages and wind up saying absolutely nothing after I cut out the fluff."

Dean Merrill, editor of *Christian Herald,* agrees. "Our taboo words are 'should/need to/ought/we must.' In the best journalistic tradition we intend to show, not tell."

And "showing" requires making good use of anecdotes and examples, those mainstays in every writer's bag of tricks. Whatever type of magazine it is—secular or inspirational—its needs are the same: a bright topic whose time has come, not come and gone; lots of quotes and "for instances"; solid background information; and an intimate writing style that lures the reader into the action and makes him care about the conclusion.

"The kiss of death in magazine publishing is to have the reader say, 'I guess that article must be for somebody else, not for somebody like me,' " says Merrill. "We cannot be satisfied with 'nice' articles. We must go for the nerve endings."

QUERIES WELCOMED

So how do you go about finding these wonderful inspirational markets that are as anxious to review your wares as you are to tout them? You have to seek them out. Most religious magazines are not on the newsstand. The library will have a modest selection, and the local Christian bookstore (depending on its size) will offer a few more. The best marketing strategy is to build a file of prospective clients by writing to publishers, requesting copies of their writers' guidelines, and sample copies of a typical issue (include cover charges and mailing fees). Names and addresses can be found in such reference resources as: *The Catholic Press Directory* (Rockville Center, N.Y.), *The Associated Church Press* (Geneva, Ill.), and *The Evangelical Press Association* (Overland Park, Kan.).

Other listings are included in *Magazine Industry Market Place, Literary Market Place, Editor and Publisher International Year Book,* and Ulrich's *International Periodicals Directory,* all published in New York City; *IMS Ayer Directory of Publications* (Fort Washington, Pa.); and *Working Press of the Nation: Volume 2, Magazine Directory* (Burlington, Iowa).

GOING ONCE, GOING TWICE . . .

Not only can the savvy writer sell to more than one periodical within the same uncommon market, but he or she can increase sales potential by expanding to other uncommon markets. For instance, good profile articles are always in demand by markets ranging from inspirational to business to hobby to professional journals. The only prerequisite to multiple sales is the writer's ability to slant the article toward each of the specialized audiences. This requires forethought prior to the interview and special questions during the course of the interview.

Example: Grammy-winning gospel singer Sandi Patti was a logical cover story for *Today's Christian Woman* and the *Christian Herald.* Each required different treatment, however, with *TCW* emphasizing Sandi's wish to blend family with career and the *Christian Herald's* focus on Sandi's favorite scriptural passage and how it has given her direction. After selling to both these inspirational markets, I looked at other specialized publications for additional sales. Since Sandi is still in her twenties and is a role model for many teenagers, I reworked the article to stress her high school and college days. *Bread* bought it. Since her family lives in the Midwest, I played up Sandi's regional roots, downplayed the religious aspect, and sold the localized version to two magazine supplements of Sunday newspapers, *The Indianapolis Star* and *Michiana. The Saturday Evening Post* then requested a national slant stressing Sandi's latest album and the resulting Grammy awards; then *The Christian Digest* bought an excerpt of the *Post* story. When my final tally was in, seven articles were the result of two brief interviews.

The secret of these successes was not only in searching for a slant, but also in looking for a link. An interview with "Garfield" creator Jim Davis reaped for me a cover story in *The Saturday Evening Post,* an excerpt in *Reader's Digest,* and a byline in a fourth-grade reading textbook published by the Charles E. Merrill Publishing Company. To be suitable for the textbook, the language had to be simplified, the sentences and paragraphs had to be shortened, but the link remained intact—kids and cats go together. This uncommon market was particularly rewarding because my words and byline were expanded to the academic field and might someday open the door at a publishing house that specializes in children's magazines.

Another uncommon market was tapped because of a commercial link. A profile of commentator Paul Harvey for *The Saturday Evening Post* led to a lucrative resale to *Carpet Retailing* magazine because Monsanto, the publication's parent company, is one of Paul Harvey's radio sponsors. Readers of *Carpet Retailing* were interested in knowing more about the man who plugs their product daily from a broadcast studio in Chicago. A specialized market? You bet, but the article required no special knowledge of floor coverings or the floor-covering business. It was a straight profile of a colorful and successful newsman.

Ditto the profile I wrote of restaurateur Bob Evans, who for nearly forty years has used sausage to bring home the bacon. The Evans article was a personality interview and was the cover story in *Right Down the Road,* a magazine published by Pioneer Hi-Bred International, Inc. (farm products) for its employees and customers. Fortunately for me, the emphasis of the article was on Evans, an entrepreneur who created an empire from a twelve-stool truckstop. I needed no expertise in seeds, sowing, or sausage. Yet the compensation was greater than most slick monthlies pay.

The lesson to be learned from these sales is this: Whenever a freelance writer interviews a notable personality, he or she should try to uncover information that might lead to sales in uncommon markets. These personalities need not be as well known as Sandi Patti, Jim Davis, Paul Harvey, or Bob Evans, but should have distinguished themselves in some way so as to be of interest to readers. Questions that might elicit valuable responses include:

In What Parts of the Country Have You Lived?
Most cities, states, and regions have publications that delight in featuring well-known "favorite sons and daughters." If your interviewee launched his career in Boston, such markets as *Boston Magazine, Yankee,* and several Sunday newspaper supplements automatically become likely targets for your queries.

What Colleges or Prep Schools Did You Attend?
Most alumni offices of colleges and universities publish prestigious quarterlies or monthlies. While pay scales will range from nonexistent to modest, getting published in these periodicals will help you in two ways. First, your list of byline credits will be expanded, and that's a major consideration for beginners. Second, some very influential people—professionals, educators, philanthropists—will be exposed to your byline. Such contacts could lead to additional opportunities.

To What Fraternal or Service Clubs Do You Belong?
All organizations, whether they are college fraternities or sororities, professional honoraries, or community service groups, have publications, and all publications need good editorial material. *The Elks Magazine, The Kiwanis Magazine, The Optimist Magazine, The Scroll* (Phi Delta Theta Greek fraternity), *The Kappan* (publication for professional educators), and scores of other specialized periodicals welcome freelance submissions.

Also included in this category are magazines geared to specific careers. Some professions boast such large memberships that their numbers can support more than one professional journal. Nursing, for instance, offers its practitioners a great deal of diversified reading, such as is found in *Nurse Educator, Nursing Outlook, Nursing Research, Nursing Life, Nursing and Health Care,* and, simply, *Nursing.*

What Are Your Hobbies?
Whatever the passion, there exists a publication to track it. *Canoe, Coin World, Lapidary Journal,* and *Model Railroader* are just a few.

ST. PETE OR BUST

Writers can tap uncommon markets with topics other than personality profiles. Any timely issue can be slanted toward a certain readership without the story losing its impact or the writer compromising any personal ethics. The author need not tell less than the whole story when writing for specialized audiences, but there must be an emphasis on the particular aspects of the story that are relevant to the special readers. For instance, subjects of interest to *Modern Maturity* subscribers are common to most publications' readers: money, health, travel, and leisure. However, given the status of *Modern Maturity* readers (retired), the emphasis will be on managing on a fixed income, maintaining wellness, destinations that cater to older vacationers (Big Band swing *vs.* Heavy Metal rock), and enjoyments that are less strenuous than marathon running and hang gliding.

SUMMARY

Article markets for the competitive writer are practically endless. Glamor may not await the contributor to *Iron Age* or *Weatherwise,* but payment does. While all writers should think big, they must also think small if they hope to thrive, not just survive. Income, bylines, career advancement, and experience are good reasons for tapping the uncommon markets. It's a strategy that makes uncommonly good sense.

Action Items

1. Come up with three strong article ideas that could be slanted toward three different *uncommon* markets.

2. Write two query letters—one to a religious magazine and one to a secular publication—proposing the same article idea, only slanting it to each magazine's particular audience.

3. Assuming your queries elicit positive replies, determine now just how your research will differ with one article directed toward an inspirational magazine and the second for general readership. How will you vary your style and tone?

Suggested Additional Readings

Writing for the Broadcast Media by Peter E. Mayeaux (Boston: Allyn and Bacon, Inc., 1985).

The Organizational Press by Lawrence Ragan (Chicago: Lawrence Ragan Communications, Inc., 1981).

Public Relations Writing Form and Style by Doug Newsom and Bob Carrell (Belmont, Calif.: Wadsworth Publishing Co., 1986).

9
Money Tactics for Becoming a Full-Time Freelancer

Reading this chapter may be worth $50,000 to you. I'm not being facetious. Stick with me and I'll prove it to you.

Let's be frank for a moment about cash. If you are like most freelance writers, you don't know any more about money management than you do about ice flow patterns in the Arctic Circle. Historically, it seems to have always been that way with writers.

Jack London earned more than a million dollars strictly from writing between 1898 and 1916, but he was never more than five thousand dollars ahead of his creditors his whole life. Mark Twain lost his fortune investing in worthless inventions. F. Scott Fitzgerald squandered his earnings and was constantly seeking loans and advances from his publisher.

In the minds of many working wordsmiths, the only way to make big bucks as a freelancer is to write a best-selling novel that later becomes a movie.

Well, that's just not so. The truth is, the total amount of money you control as a writer is in direct proportion to how you handle your writing income. If you earn five thousand dollars annually as a part-time writer and are able to invest it so that it returns to you as twenty thousand dollars, you will be farther ahead than a novelist who receives an advance of twenty thousand dollars but loses it all to taxes, lawyers, literary agents, and general expenses.

REALIZING YOUR DREAM

I've met hundreds of part-time writers who have told me, "My dream is to one day have enough money to quit my job and to go into freelance writing full time."

When I was eighteen that was my dream, too. I planned to make it by age thirty. It didn't happen until I was thirty-three, but, trust me, I've got no complaints. It's a fantastic life. I call my own hours, travel the world over (Red China and Hong Kong one year, Hawaii and New York the next year), meet famous people, own two homes, send my children to private school, and have a beautiful office. And it isn't because I'm such a fabulous writer; it's because I've learned how to manage (and leverage) my money.

Let's suppose that you are a thirty-two-year-old person, married, the parent of two children, and you are earning $3,000 to $7,000 per year as a part-time writer. Your goal is to be so financially secure in ten years you will be able to enter freelance writing on a full-time basis. (Michener didn't go full time until age forty-two, so why not you?) Now, how can you make this dream come true?

There are three ways to increase your total amount of money: earn more; preserve more; and/or leverage your money to earn more money. To become financially strong, you'll want to optimize all three of these methods. Here are some procedures to follow in doing so:

Step 1: *Borrow Short Term, Invest Long Term.*
If your credit is good, go to your local bank and borrow $3,000 for thirty-six months. Most people can get that amount as a noncollateralized "signature" loan. Take the $3,000 and invest it in a 10-year Investment Note (see sidebar), which compounds interest until it is redeemed or reaches maturity.

Here's what happens: You've borrowed $3,000 at, say, 13.5 percent interest. The payments are $101.80 per month for thirty-six months. Because part of your monthly payments goes against the principal, your loan only costs you a total of $664.80. Meanwhile, however, you have invested the $3,000 for ten years at, say, 14.65 percent interest in a long-range Investment Note, which you later cash in for $12,480.

At the end of ten years, here's the difference:

Amount borrowed	$ 3,000.00 (at 13.5%)
Interest paid	664.80 (over 3 years)
Total amount repaid	$ 3,664.80
Amount invested	$ 3,000.00 (at 14.65%)
Amount redeemed	$12,480.00 (after 10 years)
Total pre-tax profit earned	$ 8,815.20

Isn't that amazing? For about an hour of paper shuffling, you can put away nearly $9,000 toward your dream goal.

And guess what? Once your 10-year Investment Note is in your hands, you can use it as collateral to get another $3,000 loan at a

---

INVESTMENT NOTES

Investment notes come in a variety of forms: treasury bills, savings bonds, certificates of deposit, mutual funds, zero coupon bonds, certificates of accrual, and capital notes. For free brochures on any or all of these investment vehicles, you may contact the following organizations:

Ashland Finance Associates
507 Plaza Building
P. O. Box 1548
Ashland, KY 41105-1548

A. G. Edwards & Sons, Inc.
One North Jefferson Street
St. Louis, MO 63103

Scudder Managed
  Municipal Bonds
175 Federal Street
Boston, MA 02110

Investment Department
People's Heritage Federal
  Savings
P. O. Box 107
Salina, KS 67402-0107

AFC Securities, inc.
250 Carpenter Freeway
P. O. Box 660047
Dallas, TX 75266-9936

Charles Schwab & Co.
101 Montgomery Street
San Francisco, CA 94104

different bank. This time, since your loan is collateralized, the loan interest rate will be substantially lower than your first loan. This means your profit margin will jump to more than $10,000 this second time.

Naturally, you will need to make sure that you can make your monthly payments during the three years needed to repay your loans. A good practice is to always pay a month in advance just in case you should ever run into a temporary cash-flow crunch. Also, if you receive a sizable payment for an article or book advance, slap it in a lump sum against your loan. This will not only save you interest costs, but will also help you pay off your loan earlier so that you can borrow another $3,000 and make another $8,000 to $10,000 profit. Some fun, eh?

By the way, if you ever catch yourself saying, "Ten years is too long to wait to earn $8,815," just ask yourself how many hours (weeks, months) you would have to spend *writing* during the next ten years to make an extra $8,815. Once you gain that perspective, you'll also gain patience. Some writers, myself included, have used this procedure to add an extra $20,000 annually to their total investment portfolio.

Step 2: *Buy Equipment with Cash.*
The 1987 revised tax law allows up to $10,000 in immediate tax deductions for business equipment; you no longer have to depreciate these items over several years. The catch is, you cannot deduct more in expenses for equipment than you earned in the same year. For example, if you spent $10,000 for a word processor, printer, modem, and computer, but you only earned $3,000 as a writer, you would only be able to deduct $3,000. However, if you earned $3,000 and you purchased a $1,000 electronic typewriter that could later also serve as a printer for your computer, you could spread your office purchases over several years, maximize their total costs as legal deductions, and eventually still wind up with the same amount of equipment. (*Note:* This does not apply to automobiles, which now must be depreciated over six years at the rates of 20 percent, 32 percent, 19 percent, 12 percent, 12 percent, and 6 percent.) When you buy business equipment, try to pay the total bill in cash and make your purchases in states with no sales taxes; nonmortgage

interest charges and sales taxes are being phased out as legal deductions.

Step 3: *Invest Using Your Children's Names.*
Any American citizen can file for a Social Security number at any age. My son and daughter had theirs before they could walk or talk, much less sign the forms. I filed on their behalf. You can do that for your children, too.

Once your children have Social Security numbers, you can buy U.S. Savings Bonds or any other investments in their names. The interest (profit) on these bonds is declared annually and added to the other income of the child. Since most children earn virtually nothing (even if they cut lawns or babysit), they are so far below the taxable income level, they get to keep the interest earned on the savings bonds *tax free*.

Each child will have to file a yearly income tax form (no real problem). The bond interest can be declared each year, or later when the bond is redeemed.

So, if you are working at the factory instead of writing because your children need band instruments, school tuition, and other "necessities," start buying them bonds or other investments. Five years from now you can quit the factory job and let the kids redeem the bonds to pay their own expenses. You'll double your money (a fifty dollar bond only costs twenty-five dollars) and it will be tax free.

Step 4: *Use Low Interest Insurance Policy Loans.*
If you don't have a strong credit rating, you can still create a pool of interest-earning capital for yourself.

Pull out your whole-life insurance policies and check the loan rates. You'll probably discover that you can borrow the cash value of the policy at only 5 to 8 percent interest. You can borrow $1,000 and then invest it in a 5-year Certificate of Deposit earning 7 to 12 percent interest at your local bank.

A $1,000 policy loan for five years at 5 percent will cost you $284.10 in interest fees, but a C.D. investment at 9 percent will earn you $560.51 in interest. You will make a profit of $276.41. If that amount seems small to you, think of it another way: If you earn twenty-five dollars a week writing a Saturday column for your local newspaper, it will take you an entire summer of column writing to earn more than $276.41. So, is it worth applying for an insurance policy loan? You bet it is!

Step 5: *Create Credit and Profit Through Shared Loans.*
If you want to increase your borrowing power while also earning some extra money, you can leverage your money through shared loans at your local lending institution.

Let's say that after making several freelance magazine article sales, you've earned about $1,150. You can take that money and put it into a savings account at a savings and loan institution or a bank near you. This savings account will only earn you about 5 to 6 percent interest, but that's not the main concern for what we have in mind.

With your money secured in the savings account, you can go to the loan officer and say that you want a "shared loan" for a thousand dollars. This means, in effect, that you want to borrow back $1,000 of your own $1,150 in your savings account.

The loan officer will then take your savings account book away from you and "freeze" your account so that no money may be withdrawn from it until you pay back the $1,000 loan. Note this, however: Even though your account is frozen, *it will still earn its regular interest* for you.

Since your $1,000 loan is secured by your savings account (and thus is no risk to the bank), you will be able to borrow the money at a discount rate. For example, if the usual rate is 13 percent interest, you will probably only have to pay 10 percent interest. Also, there's no time limit on this kind of loan. As long as you pay the quarterly interest premiums, your shared loan can go on virtually indefinitely.

So, with your borrowed thousand dollars, you can purchase a 10-year Capital Note at a rate of, say, 11 percent. Now notice what has happened here: You have borrowed at 10 percent, but you are now simultaneously earning at 6 percent and at 11 percent . . . and it's all *the same $1,000.*

Over a ten-year period, your $1,000 loan at 10 percent will cost you $1,685.06 in interest. Invested at 17 percent interest (6% + 11%), however, it will earn you $4,101.08. That's a pre-tax profit margin of $2,416.02—and that's per $1,000 invested. Obviously, if you could leverage as much as $5,000 in this procedure, your profit would jump to more than $12,000. And that ain't hay. (*Note:* Single premium whole-life insurance policies can be used for this procedure, too.)

Step 6: *Open an Individual Retirement Account.*
Since the basic purpose of this chapter has been to teach you how to be financially able to go full time on your own as a freelancer after ten years of planning, you may wonder why I might suggest opening an IRA. It's because of the tax benefits. Whereas the *earnings* from an IRA cannot be enjoyed until a person reaches age 59½, the *tax benefits* are useful *now*. And since preserving income is one of the ways to make money, that's important to you.

In 1987, the tax laws were revised in regard to IRAs. Any couple filing a joint return of $40,000 or less can now invest and deduct $2,000 per year per working person or $2,250 per married couple with one unemployed spouse. Couples earning between $40,000 and $50,000 are prorated according to their exact income. (For example, a couple earning a total of $45,000 with one spouse enrolled in a qualified retirement plan at his or her place of employment would only be eligible for 50 percent of the normal IRA deduction allowances.) Individuals or couples earning more than $50,000 annually may fund an IRA to its $2,000 (single) or $4,000 (working couple) maximum, and the interest and dividends may be tax deferred until they are withdrawn after age 59½; however, the $2,000 or $4,000 amounts are not tax deductible the way they are for persons earning less than $40,000 annually. If you have an IRA established during a year when you suddenly become flush with money (after receiving a heavy advance on a book contract or getting paid in advance for a year's worth of monthly columns), you'll have some way of sheltering some of this cash.

Bernard Baruch once described compound interest as "the eighth wonder of the world." Truly, money when invested and managed properly can be a wondrous thing. It can work as effectively for you as it often does against you.

This minicourse in cash management is meant to serve only as an eye-opener to the many options available to anyone who is determined one day to become financially able to enter writing on a full-time basis. Your family accountant or certified financial planner will be able to show you other ways to maximize the use of your funds.

Money management takes discipline, patience, and some element of risk. But the fact is, it can make dreams come true.

Besides making money, you will also need to know how to control, manage, shelter, and save your money. One way to go about this is to become a one-person corporation, as I did. Let me explain the procedure.

WRITERS AS CORPORATIONS

To most people, I am Dennis E. Hensley, magazine columnist and book author. But not to my accountant. To him, I'm Denehen, Incorporated, a freelance writing business with a home office (a literal term) in Fort Wayne, Indiana. (Denehen stands for *Den*nis *E. Hens*ley.)

Whereas becoming a one-person corporation may not be right for every freelance writer, I can attest to the fact that it has saved me thousands of tax dollars. A sole proprietor (single person) who earns more than $16,800 annually (or $28,000 as a married person filing a joint tax return) will be taxed at 15 percent; however, a writer who is incorporated can earn up to $50,000 before his or her corporation is taxed at 15 percent.

Let's note the difference. Suppose two writers each earn $50,000. Author A is not incorporated, so he/she must pay 35 percent of this money in taxes. Author B, however, is incorporated and arranges for the corporation to pay him/her only $16,800 in annual salary and to use the balance of funds for "expenses and benefits" for the author (business travel, office rent, new computer and word processor, insurance coverage, retirement plan, personal publicity and advertising, phone bills, and writing supplies). Author B will pay $14,980 less in taxes than Author A. Even if Author A has a variety of legitimate deductions, the difference in tax payments will still be many thousands of dollars.

The real determining factor regarding whether or not to incorporate will be your "bottom line" net income or loss. For example, if you earn far less than $16,800 as a single writer and you have considerable deductions—say, for equipment like a typewriter or word processor or file cabinets—that reduce your taxable income, there probably would be no need to incorporate. Those expenses would already be sheltering much of your personal income. However, if you need additional deductions, incorporating would help you. Let me explain how.

As a sole proprietor, you can deduct 25 percent of your health insurance premiums for yourself and your dependents unless your spouse's health insurance covers your entire family. You can also deduct the cost of the writers' trade magazines you subscribe to and most of the writers' conferences you attend. However, as a self-employed person you can only deduct work-related expenses for meals and your automobile if they exceed 2 percent of your adjusted gross income. If your publisher reimburses you for expenses, you may not deduct those costs. No business-related trips may be deducted if any parts of the trips were for vacations, too.

Whereas a corporation can deduct the full cost of maintaining a writing office (my corporation pays me a hundred dollars per month as "rent" for the room I use in my home as a writing office), a sole proprietor can only deduct the costs of maintaining a home office from his or her *net* earnings as a writer. For example, if you earn $4,000 as a freelance writer and have $1,500 in general expenses, the most you can deduct for home office expenses is $2,500.

Incorporated writers are able to deduct their medical and dental costs and disability and life insurance premiums with pre-tax dollars. The corporation simply offers these benefits to all its employees (which usually consists of just the writer) and the corporation deducts them "off the top" as business expenses. Sole proprietor writers must pay for these benefits with after-tax dollars, and even then, many of these benefits are only deductible to the 25 percent limit.

In the case of life insurance, a writer who is a sole proprietor cannot take the cost of his premiums as a tax deduction, but a corporation can provide up to $50,000 of coverage for a person and the premiums are 100 percent deductible. Although medical and dental costs and insurance premiums *may* be deducted by individuals if these expenses exceed 7½ percent of the person's adjusted gross income, very few people ever qualify for such deductions.

With a corporation, however, such expenses are 100 percent deductible.

A corporation can establish a SEPP-IRA qualified retirement plan for employees and thus allow the writer/employee to channel up to 15 percent of gross earnings (or $30,000, whichever is less) into this tax-deferred account. Additionally, the writer may be able to put another $2,000 (depending on the income range earnings, as I explained earlier in this chapter) annually into a personal IRA. Sole proprietor writers have the IRA option, or a Keogh plan. If an incorporated writer earns $20,000 annually, he or she can have the corporation set aside $3,000 in a retirement fund (15 percent of $20,000); the writer then can place another $2,000 into a private IRA (subject to income limitations). Thus, up to $5,000 of the writer's income could be saved, invested, and sheltered from taxation.

GETTING STARTED

It is often less difficult to become incorporated than most writers imagine. Several states, such as Indiana where I incorporated, do not even require that a lawyer be hired to complete the paperwork.

By writing to the Secretary of State of your state, you can receive the appropriate forms and information. Simply ask for an incorporation checklist and an application to file articles of incorporation. The incorporation fee is usually very modest; in Michigan it costs thirty-five dollars; in Indiana it costs thirty-six dollars; other states are in this range.

There is usually a "minimum capital" requirement also. This means that your corporation must be worth a minimum amount of money right from the start. In Indiana, for example, a corporation must be valued at a minimum of one thousand dollars. This figure is arrived at by adding your available corporate cash to the value of your contributing assets. If you have $250 in cash and $750 in equipment, software, and office furniture, you will have reached the minimum capital level.

Using an attorney (which I feel is safest), you should expect to pay not more than $500 to $1,000 for incorporation filing assistance.

Call several attorneys, shop around, and establish the fees in advance.

For your payments, you should expect four services:

1. One or two consultations with the lawyer regarding incorporation procedures
2. Full preparation by the attorney of your articles of incorporation
3. Assistance with your initial stockholders' meeting after your charter is received from the state, as well as help with your first board of directors' meeting, wherein officers are elected. (*Note:* The writer can personally hold all officer and board seats.)
4. Providing a corporate minutes book with stock certificates

Regarding records, your corporation will need to keep a general ledger, a cash receipts journal, a cash disbursements journal, and a payroll journal.

I would suggest that you hire a local accountant to set up your books and to instruct you on how to fill them out. Afterward, a semiannual visit to your accountant will ensure that you are on track with your record-keeping and that you are advised of any new laws or procedural changes the government has enacted. You should become familiar with payroll tax forms and either fill them out yourself or have your accountant handle them on a quarterly basis.

Together you and your accountant can make sure that you have properly paid state and federal withholding taxes, state unemployment taxes, FICA (Social Security), FUTA (federal unemployment taxes), and state sales tax (if you direct-market any of your books to customers), and that you have filled out your Form 1120, which is the annual corporate income tax return.

This may seem like a lot of paperwork, and it is. However, these tax payments are now credited to your benefit in reducing your taxable income, whereas previously they were simply taken out of your gross earnings. The difference is substantial: A sole proprietor writer earning $50,000 would pay $13,889 in taxes, whereas an incorporated writer would only pay $8,250 (a savings of $5,639 every year).

One note of caution: Make sure that all of your writing assignments and agreements are between the client and your corporation, not you personally. Otherwise, the earnings will be subject to ordinary *personal* income tax rates. This is commonly referred to as the "PHC trap" (wherein you are assumed to be an operator of a personal holding company). This area should be reviewed at the beginning of your incorporation procedure by your attorney; he or she should prepare a standard contract that will accomplish this. Remember—a client should not mention you specifically in a contract, even though you actually will be doing the work.

With taxes spiraling higher and higher all the time, the modern freelance writer must be cognizant of every legal maneuver available for preserving income. Incorporating is one of the safest ways to achieve income protection.

Action Items

1. Figure out how much you are worth per hour as a freelance writer. Think about the last piece of writing you sold. Add together the number of hours it took you to research the piece; add on the hours it took you to write your rough and final drafts; finally, add on the hours it took you to type and mail the piece. Now take that total number of hours and divide it into the amount of money you earned for the piece. That's how much you are worth per hour as a writer.

2. Write out your ten-year goals as a writer. If a book is in your plans, in what year will it be published? Will it be a novel or a work of nonfiction? How will you prepare yourself for this challenge? Will you need more schooling? Should you attend more writers' conferences? Will you be ready for a literary agent two years from now? Be as specific as possible in setting your goals.

3. Set up a basic bookkeeping system that will help you keep track of your expenses in developing your career as a writer. Also keep a record of your earnings as a writer. Compare the two amounts each quarter to gauge your financial progress.

Suggested Additional Readings

The Courage to Be Rich by Mark O. Haroldsen (New York: G. P. Putnam's Sons, 1983).

How to Borrow Your Way to a Great Fortune by Tyler G. Hicks (West Nyack, N.Y.: Reward Books, 1970).

Financial Stability for Today's Christians by Dennis E. Hensley (Anderson, Ind.: Warner Press, 1987).

How to Get Happily Published by Judith Appelbaum and Nancy Evans (New York: Harper & Row, 1978).

The Power of Money Dynamics by Venita Van Caspel (New York: Simon and Schuster, 1983).

10

The Questions Asked Most Frequently About Authorship

Last chapter.

Last chance for a remaining question.

Whenever we design a day-long writers' workshop for a group, we try to anticipate participants' needs. And wants. We take into account the changing market, new tastes of readers, new trends of publishers, and special interests of writers. If a Detroit audience wants to talk poetry, poetry it is; if children's fiction is the burning issue in Kansas City, we'll work it into the schedule. No two seminars are the same, and even though we build in a certain amount of "stretch" to accommodate a group's uniqueness, sometimes even we are surprised at the diverse wiggles a workshop can take.

One element is always constant, though: the questions. At the end of the day we always set aside time for those final before-you-go-away questions, the answers to which were somehow overlooked during the regular work sessions. Inevitably, one question leads to another and often only the threat of a missed plane brings closure.

While two-way dialogue is impossible in book format, last-minute questions are too important to omit. Many questions are predictable—they surface at nearly every seminar—and so we've put together our Top Twenty. These are the twenty most frequently asked questions, complete with answers of course.

Ready for the count-down?

Q. *I've heard the expression that a beginning freelancer has to pay his dues. What does that mean?*

A. Seldom does a newcomer sell the first bit of writing he submits.

(Exceptions exist, of course: Michael Crichton, author of *The Andromeda Strain*, sold a travel piece to *The New York Times* at age fourteen.) At first, the beginner might receive a string of rejection slips, followed by a sale, followed by another string of rejection slips. Often, as he endures this rejection period, he is said to be paying his dues. Certainly there's nothing that says you have to pay dues at all. It's what you learn from your rejections that's important, not the number you accumulate. You need to ask yourself, Why was this query idea vetoed by the editor? Was it the idea? Was it the way I presented the idea? Or did I present a good idea but to the wrong market?

Q. How many times must a manuscript be rejected before you chalk it up to experience and tuck it in the bottom drawer?
A. If you believe in a manuscript, you should keep submitting it until you run out of publishing houses. And then start over. If the pages become dog-eared, take the advice of a prolific freelancer I know: She *irons* the top sheet before sending a rejected manuscript on to the next market. You're in good company if your manuscript has earned at least one or two passovers. Among well-known books that have been rejected on their way to fame and fortune are *The Peter Principle* (thumbs down more than a dozen times), *Lord of the Flies, Love Story, Jonathan Livingston Seagull, A Separate Peace, The Godfather*, and *Auntie Mame*.

Q. I'm just getting serious about freelance writing and wonder how much money I should invest in the business. What tools do I need to buy?
A. As few as possible. Obviously, you're going to have to have access to a typewriter or someone who is willing to type for you, because under no circumstances should you ever submit a handwritten manuscript to an editor. We recommend a typewriter that can accommodate a one-time-use film ribbon for finished manuscripts and a fabric ribbon for first drafts. If you're going to do interviews, you might consider a small, inexpensive cassette tape recorder and a couple of one-hour tapes. Be sure you have an adaptor for the recorder so you can plug it in and not depend on expensive batteries. A good dictionary is the cornerstone of a writer's library.

Also useful are a thesaurus, a pocket almanac for miscellaneous facts, and a paperback grammar primer in case you're rusty on rules of punctuation. A supply of paper, pens, envelopes, and stamps is all you need to launch your business. Later, you might consider investing some of your profit in mailing labels, business cards, and a word processor. All are worthwhile purchases but certainly aren't necessary to success.

Q. *I have a hard time distinguishing between a short-short story, a short story, and a novelette. Any guidelines?*
A. A short-short story ranges from 500 to 2,000 words or, roughly, from two to eight typewritten pages; a short story is usually from 2,500 to 5,000 words, which translates to ten to twenty pages; and a novelette is 7,000 to 15,000 words, or twenty-eight to sixty pages.

Q. *How about a book? How much longer is a book-length manuscript?*
A. That depends on what kind of book you're writing. For instance, a paperback book might run from 35,000 to 80,000 words. I have a friend who is a very successful romance writer under contract to Harlequin and her manuscripts have to be as close to two hundred pages as she can come. On the other hand, a hard-cover novel can range up to 150,000 words or more. Of course, children's books might have as few as 500 words.

Q. *I'm interested in writing humor. Tips, please.*
A. Mark Twain once said, "There are several kinds of stories, but only one difficult kind to write, and that's the humorous." Humor is tough because it's so fragile. Some humor doesn't live very long, especially if it's tied to something very contemporary, like a well-known person or an event that's in the headlines right now. Art Buchwald, who writes political satire, told me once during an interview that whenever he sifts through his past columns looking for the best ones to include in an anthology, he's struck by the fact that some of the funniest have lost their humor since they were written. Times change, news events are forgotten, and the humor attached to them is gone.

Remember that there are different types of humor—dry, wry,

witty, caustic, subtle, slapstick, situation comedy, and one-liners. It's possible to read an entire book of humor and truly enjoy it without letting out a single belly laugh.

Whatever your specialty, here are a few guidelines that might help in writing humor:

- Keep it short. Trim your text to the minimum. Leave your readers wanting more. Remember, most humor columns are less than a thousand words.
- Keep cool. Sometimes, taking a witty stand on a hot issue can produce great copy that readers relate to (politics, fashion, women's lib). But be careful if your topic is too close to you. Don't get so fired up that you lose control and reach the boiling point. Your humor may melt away.
- Keep up. Don't slip into cliché humor. Some of the early TV sitcoms centered on stereotypes—women who lacked brains (*I Love Lucy*) or bumbling blue-collar types (*The Honeymooners, Life of Riley*). They are classics; but you're contemporary. Make sure you have a new angle if you're reviving a tired joke.

Probably the best advice is to keep the humor believable. There's a fine line between funny and silly. At the heart of all humor is a seed of truth. If you read current humorists, you'll see that they usually base their zaniness on fact. Art Buchwald will take something from the newspaper and embroider it. And once he starts embroidering, no one is immune to his needle. ("All my columns are based on truth," he told me. "That's what makes them work.") Erma Bombeck takes situations we've all experienced and runs with them. ("Basically, I'm not funny," she insisted during an interview we did over breakfast one morning in Chicago. "When you've been doing this as long as I have, you learn to appreciate humor and you look for it all the time.")

Most publications welcome good humor. It's always in demand, probably because there isn't enough to go around. It can't be manufactured; it has to be observed and recorded.

Q. *I know I want to write, but I don't have time. What can I do now in order to prepare myself for when my children are older and I'm able to start creating the stories that I know are inside me?*

A. F. Scott Fitzgerald's advice was to "absorb half a dozen top-flight authors every year." But do you have time? Keeping a journal of your thoughts and feelings is a good idea, but do you have time? I'm reminded of Marabel Morgan, who wrote *The Total Woman* (don't snicker; it was the runaway best-seller of 1974, outdistancing *All the President's Men* by some 100,000 copies). When asked how she wrote her book while caring for a four-year-old daughter and a new baby, she explained that she did it in fifteen-second intervals, scribbling her thoughts on yellow legal sheets and pasting them together during nap period. Not a bad idea. But do you have time? My point is pointed: If you truly want to write, you don't find time, you make time.

Q. *As a writer, am I obliged to let the person I've interviewed read my article before it is published?*
A. Absolutely not. If a person has granted you an interview and knew when he granted it that it was destined for print, he has already given you permission to publish his comments. You're a professional and he must trust you to practice your craft free of censorship.

If you agree to let a source read your story, you run the risk of having him tamper with your style, change quotes he might have second thoughts about, and remove the article's life and flair. You actually forfeit your independence, and that is something a writer values very much.

The only time I ever have agreed to let someone read my manuscript is when the topic is filled with technical material I'm not entirely sure I understand. The person is then allowed only to check facts, not change words.

Q. *I'm trying to make the switch from nonfiction to fiction, but I'm having trouble with creating believable characters. What am I doing wrong?*
A. When you write nonfiction, you observe your characters; when you write fiction, you have to create them, and this takes a bit more thought and planning. Remember that you can reveal your characters to your readers in several different ways. One way is to come right out and physically describe each of them. When you do this, think of your senses. Your eyes will tell what the character looks like; your ears will tell what kind of a voice he has; your sense of smell will pick up on his after-shave lotion or other scents. Even

your sense of touch can reveal important clues, such as the firmness of his grip or whether his hands are calloused or soft.

You can also describe a character through his dialogue or by the way secondary characters respond to him. You can describe him through his actions: by the way he walks (does he strut, swagger or lope?); by the way he sits (does he slouch, cross his legs, or grip the arms of the chair with white knuckles?).

Think through your character until you know him like a best friend. Give him words to speak, thoughts to think. Take him through an uneventful day. After you get to know him, *really* know him, he'll come alive on paper because he'll seem alive in your imagination.

Q. *I have an idea for a weekly column. How can I get it syndicated?*
A. Competition is fierce, unfortunately. To give you an idea just how fierce it is, currently there are some forty syndicated health columns, seventy-five religious features, and about twelve columns on stamp collecting available! The best way to break into the syndicated marketplace is through your local newspaper. Convince the editor to run your column and test its audience appeal. If you get some response, ask the editor to offer the column to a syndicate he buys material from. You'll need to have several weeks' worth of samples to prove that you can sustain your theme over the long haul.

Cartoonist Jim Davis once gave me insight into just how difficult it is to have material syndicated. During an interview, he told me of the years he spent trying to interest a syndicate in his strip called "Gnorm the Gnat." He even gave the strip to a small weekly newspaper in central Indiana in order to build a following for the pesky little bug. No luck. It wasn't until he did an in-depth study of the marketplace (there are more than 250 comic strips available) to learn what was lacking that he came up with a winner. Enter Garfield.

Q. *I'm beginning to sell on a regular basis to regional publications such as the Sunday magazine supplement to our newspaper and to the city magazine in our state capital. I'm amazed, however, at how little I am paid. Is this subject to negotiation? How could a full-time freelancer support himself?*

A. Small publications usually operate on tight budgets and thus have fixed rates to pay writers. Often this amounts to little more than 10 cents a word. If you're just starting out, consider your work as an investment in the future. Sure, you're not getting rich, but you're getting bylines that may boost you into larger markets. Don't be content to limit yourself to these small magazines. As soon as you have acquired a few good clips, start sending them out with query letters to editors of larger publications. Use your clips to prove your ability. Once you've graduated to better-paying periodicals, start eyeing even larger markets.

Q. *What about expense money? Can I expect to be reimbursed for long distance telephone calls, trips out of town, and photography costs?*
A. Yes, but make sure such details are worked out when you accept an assignment. Keep a careful and accurate log of your expenditures. The accepted rate is 21 cents per mile now for travel, and many new cars are equipped with trip gauges to make your record-keeping easier. Compile your receipts for meals, lodging, phone calls, copy machine costs, film, and tapes, attach the sales slips to a typed listing of your expenses, and include this with your finished manuscript.

Q. *What is my time worth? Some articles simply take longer to produce than others. Can I expect a higher fee?*
A. Many magazines operate strictly on a per-word basis. Others are willing to adjust payment for special circumstances. For example, Rich Willowby, managing editor of *Vital Christianity*, recently told me that he likes to quote a per-story rather than a per-word payment. He is sensitive to the fact that some articles require hours of research in the library, and these hours do not necessarily show up on an expense account. Other assignments, particularly those expressing an opinion, can be written without the writer ever leaving his office.

If you anticipate that an article is going to necessitate an unusual investment of time, negotiate for a higher fee *before* accepting the assignment. You'll have more leverage at that point rather than after the fact.

Q. *I've been performing a "balancing act" for several years: I work by day, write by night. When can I safely plunge into full-time writing?*

A. Full-time freelancer Michael Banks once advised in a *Writer's Digest* article to wait until your writing income equals about half of your job income. He suggests that if you are writing an average of fifteen hours a week but you're not earning half of your job income, you're probably not ready to make the switch.

Cash flow inconsistency and lack of structure in your day may be the most difficult adjustments to make to the full-time writing life. Tyndale House editor Virginia Muir urges writers to put their shoes on. What she means, of course, is that writing is a profession just like any other. Practitioners should prepare for their professional day just as other professionals do—get up, get dressed, put on their makeup, put on their shoes, and go to the office . . . even if the office doubles as the spare bedroom or the breakfast nook.

Q. *Interviewing celebrities sounds great, but what celebrity is going to grant an interview to an unknown writer whose article may never be published?*

A. No celebrity is likely to give his valuable time without some assurance of a return on his investment. But you, the writer, can get around this easily.

First, consider offering your writing talent to the local newspaper as a stringer. This merely means that when the editor has an overabundance of assignments, he will call you to help. You may have to cover a school board meeting in a nearby suburb, or you may be sent to interview a town marshal twenty miles up the road in order to boost the newspaper's rural circulation. But—and here's your payback—the affiliation can work to your advantage when a celebrity is in the area. Tell your editor that you'd like to try to schedule an interview. If you've earned your stripes covering the mundane stories, he'll probably encourage you to go for the plum. When you contact the celebrity's agent or road manager, you can honestly say you represent the local newspaper. Thus, the personality has assurance that the interview will result in exposure for him in a market he plans to visit. After you fulfill your obligation to supply the newspaper with a story, you are free to recycle the interview material into a magazine article.

Or try a different tack. If you find that a celebrity is going to be in your city, write a query letter to a national publication offering a profile of the personality. When the editor bites, contact the celebrity's agent or road manager, identify yourself as a freelance writer and explain that a magazine has asked you to submit an article on the celebrity. This should land you the interview, and then it's up to you to turn the interview into a sale.

Q. *What's your prescription for chronic writer's block?*
A. If you're prone to bouts with this persistent malady, plan ahead. Keep a list of article and story ideas to refer to when creative juices run dry. Clip interesting items from the newspaper so when the words don't flow at the typewriter you can review the clips, schedule interviews, and at least accomplish the legwork required for a new story. Perhaps by the time you've completed the research you'll be ready to put thoughts to paper again.

Dorothy Hamilton, a farm wife who launched her career as a prolific novelist after the age of sixty, once shared with me her antidote for writer's block. She claimed that if you made writing a habit, creativity would become a habit as well. She used to write in the early morning hours—a throwback to her active farming days—and always would sit in a hard, straight-back chair. She used a lapboard, wrote in longhand on yellow legal pads with a fountain pen filled with black ("It couldn't be blue," she specified) ink. She did this so regularly that when she sat down in that same chair in that same place at the same time every morning, the words flowed easily, black ink on yellow paper.

Another writer, this one a creator of western fiction, set aside two hours every evening at the kitchen table. He disciplined himself to stay there from 7 to 9 p.m. or until he had completed two pages of finished text—whichever came first.

Or you can follow the system of the German poet and dramatist Friedrich Von Schiller, who used to keep rotting apples under the lid of his desk because he claimed their smell helped him to write. (I'll opt for penance at the kitchen table or in the straight-back chair at 5 a.m. any day.)

Q. *Most writers have trouble coming up with bright beginnings. My problem is at the opposite end: I don't know when or where to stop. Suggestions?*
A. Whether you write fiction or nonfiction, know before you start where you are going to end up. Decide first on a conclusion and then view it like a target, aiming everything toward it. In fiction, you don't have to tie together each detail into a happy-ever-after ending. Who would believe such a story? The only requirement for a good ending in fiction is that the main characters shouldn't be quite the same at the conclusion as they were at the beginning. In nonfiction, the last paragraph can be a simple restatement of the article's point, a final quote that sums up the point, or one last anecdote that illustrates the point.

Q. *How can I broaden my ability? Everything I write—fiction, nonfiction, humor, and essays—seems to sound the same.*
A. Every writer reaches plateaus in his career, times when he questions whether or not he is growing in his art. James Thurber, at age fifty-nine, wrote: "With sixty staring me in the face, I have developed inflammation of the sentence structure and a definite hardening of the paragraphs."

Don't become too introspective about your foibles. A writer has a style as identifiable as a singer's. Rather than trying to change it, why not concentrate on refining it? Know what you do well and strive to do it better. Be a specialist. That is not to say you shouldn't experiment, but fine-tune your special skill to excellence. Consider it a compliment if a reader, without benefit of byline, recognizes a piece of writing as your own.

Q. *I never went to college, I haven't traveled much, I haven't had what you would call an exciting life. Am I presumptuous to think I can be a professional writer?*
A. Gore Vidal never graduated from college, and Agatha Christie hardly went to school at all. Emily Dickinson rarely left her house in Amherst and Elizabeth Barrett Browning seldom budged from her fainting couch. Don't make the mistake of thinking you have to have endured three world wars, a divorce and two "out-of-body" experiences to have sufficient "material" to write. As mystery queen

Christie once said, "The best time for planning a book is while you're doing the dishes."

Q. *Still, before I begin sending manuscripts to editors I want more training. Where can I get it?*
A. A lot depends on how much you want to invest—in terms of money and time. Subscribe to a good writers' magazine; check the card file at your library for books geared to writers. You'll find material addressing every kind of writing, from children's series to greeting card messages. Consider attending a writers' conference. Some are scheduled for a day at a time, a weekend, or an entire week. Most will feature writers who candidly share their expertise with beginners and intermediates. You'll meet other people like yourself and make contact with several professionals.

Be aware of writers who visit your town and give lectures. Often local libraries sponsor lecture series and charge little, if anything, for admission. You'll benefit not only from their prepared remarks but from rubbing elbows afterward over punch and cookies. More contacts.

Check with a college in your area for a listing of its writing classes. Many of these are offered on credit or noncredit bases. I guarantee you won't feel intimidated. I've taught a creative writing course for years as part of the adult education program at a Big Ten university. My students have ranged from a podiatrist to a truck driver to a retiree to a radio deejay. Interestingly, the truck driver had more talent than the professionals.

Many communities have writers' clubs or discussion groups. Pick one that challenges you to stretch in order to keep up.

But one last word of advice: Don't spend all of your time going about the business of *becoming* a writer. Set aside most of your writing time for actual writing. Don't be a writer who wants to have written; be a writer who wants to write.

Glossary of Freelance Writing Terms

For those freelance writers who may not be familiar with all the terminology used in magazines and books on freelance writing, this alphabetized list will provide definitions commonly used in the world of publishing.

Advance. When an author signs a book contract with a publisher, the publisher usually pays the author an "advance" against future royalties. For example, if the publisher pays the author a thousand-dollar advance, that amount is later deducted from the author's royalties until it is worked off.

Author's Representative. An author's representative (or "literary agent," as he or she is more commonly called) is a person who represents an author in negotiating publishing contracts, paperback resales, overseas rights, and work-made-for-hire assignments. Lists of current literary agents may be obtained from The Writers' Guild of America, West 8955 Beverly Blvd., Los Angeles, California 90048; and from The Society of Authors' Representatives, 39½ Washington Square South, New York, New York 10012. An agent's rates should be 10 percent on domestic sales and 20 percent on foreign sales.

Clippings/Tearsheets. A sample of an author's writing that has been clipped from a periodical (clipping) or torn from a sheet of a newspaper (tearsheet) is often sent along with a query letter as a way of displaying a writer's credentials.

Co-Author. When two writers work together to write an article or book, they are considered joint creators, or "co-authors," of the finished piece of writing. Usually, both their names appear in the byline and they split the payment or royalties equally.

Credits Sheet. A credits sheet is a listing of all (for a novice writer) or select prestige markets (for an experienced writer) where the author has been published. Book publishers frequently wish to review a writer's credit sheet before risking a cash advance for a book project.

Expense Fees. If a nonfiction freelance writer is hired by a magazine to travel to a distant location in order to cover a story or conduct an interview, the freelancer should ask for "expense fees" to cover his or her airfare, gas and mileage, meals, lodging, and other costs incurred while in pursuit of the story.

Front/Back-of-the-Book Features. Most large staff-written national magazines have regular short features or rotating columns, in front or back of each issue, that are open to freelance writers.

Ghostwriter. Whenever a professional writer is hired to write a book that will bear another person's name as author, the real writer is called a ghostwriter. His or her name will not appear on the book. Ghostwriters are usually used when a well-known person wishes to write his or her autobiography, yet that person lacks the polished writing skills to make the book read well.

Hook. All articles and interviews need some sort of news peg or special slant that will attract a reader's attention. These leads are called hooks (or angles) because they figuratively snag the reader's interest.

In-House Operation. An in-house prepared magazine is one prepared by a hired staff, and therefore uses no freelance material. An in-house publication is a magazine or tabloid prepared for workers of a particular company or corporation.

Journalese. Journalese is an umbrella term for all slang expressions or trade jargon associated with a newspaper.

Kill Fee. If an author is given an assignment and is promised to be paid a set fee upon satisfactory acceptance of his or her manuscript, he or she is also guaranteed a kill fee in case the editor or publisher does not choose to use the completed manuscript. For example, if a writer is hired to write a freelance article for payment of $1,000, with a kill fee of 35 percent, the editor will have to pay the writer $350 even if the editor chooses to reject or not use the finished article.

Lead. The lead (or lede) comes from the typesetting term *leder lines,* meaning the opening sentences of a story or article. A lead must grab the attention of the reader and make him or her want to read the entire article.

Marketing. When an author seeks a publisher or periodical to purchase and print his or her manuscripts, the author is "marketing" his or her material; however, to a publisher, "marketing" is the process of planning a sales strategy for selling the book to readers, i.e., distribution, cover design, publicity.

Ms./Mss. The abbreviation *ms.* stands for manuscript, meaning the typed version of an article or book or short story as it is sent from the author to the editor or publisher. The plural form is *mss.*

Net to Author. In negotiating a book contract, a publisher will usually offer a royalty arrangement that begins with 10 percent earnings for the author. It is up to the author or the literary agent to pin down in a contract if that means 10 percent of the cover price (retail) or of the price of the book for the bookstore (wholesale) or of whatever the total earnings of the book are for the publisher (including volume discounts, remainders, and promotional copies). The ultimate actual cash that must be paid to the writer is the *net to author* agreement between the author and publisher.

Op-Ed. The sections of newspapers or magazines in which the "opinion" columns and "editorials" appear are known as the op-ed pages.

O.P. When a reader orders a book from a publisher and receives a notice that the book is O.P., it means the book is *out of print;* it is no longer being published.

Over the Transom. In past eras, editors used to work in office buildings that had an open frosted window (a transom) above their office entrance door. Since manuscripts in large envelopes could not fit through the small mail slot cut into the outer door, the postman would toss the manuscripts over the transom and let them fall into the office. Later, the term *over the transom* came to mean manuscripts that arrived unsolicited.

Pen Name/Pseudonym. When an author uses a name other than his own for the byline of his articles or books, the fictitious name is called a pen name or pseudonym. The pen name of Samuel L. Clemens was Mark Twain. The pen name of Evan Hunter was Ed McBain. The pen name of H. H. Munro was Saki.

Paragraph Rate. Rather than paying a by-the-word rate for free-lance material, some magazines pay so much per paragraph or so much per column inch or so much per page. Financially, this usually is to the author's disadvantage.

Payment upon Acceptance. With a *payment upon acceptance* agreement, an editor pays an author for a freelance article as soon as the editor accepts the article for publication. Most authors insist on this arrangement.

Payment upon Publication. With a *payment upon publication* agreement, the author receives no money for his or her article or short story until after it has been printed in the accepting magazine and distributed to the newsstands and subscribers. Thus if an article is accepted in January and published in December, it will be a year or more before the author receives any payment or is able to attempt to remarket that manuscript to another publication.

Query Letter. A *query* (or questioning) *letter* is a one-page, single-spaced letter sent to an editor outlining the idea an author has for a potential article. The query asks the editor if he or she would be interested in reading or buying such an article.

SASE. All query letters and manuscripts should be sent with a self-addressed, stamped envelope (SASE) on the inside, which the editor can use to reply to you at no expense to the magazine or book company you are contacting.

Sidebar. Any ancillary information that assists an article but is not put into the body of the article (such as a list of addresses or a sample quiz) can be set off in a box and printed alongside the article.

Spec/Speculation. If an editor receives an interesting query letter from a writer he has never heard of, he may request that the author submit his or her manuscript *on spec*, meaning on speculation. If the editor likes it, he will buy it; if the editor does not like it, the manuscript will be rejected and no kill fee will be paid. After an author has sold material to a publication and has thus established credibility, it is no longer proper for an editor to ask to see things on spec. The editor should either reject the query idea or make an assignment for the article and establish a kill fee for it.

Think Piece. Essays and analytical articles that require some above-average concentration from the reader are termed *think pieces* by editors. Often, guest editorials fall into this category.

Unsolicited. If a writer sends a manuscript to an editor without first having solicited the editor's permission to submit the manuscript (via a query letter), that submission is known as an *unsolicited manuscript*. Some periodicals have a policy against accepting unsolicited material and will send the submissions back unopened.

Index

About the Authors

DENNIS E. HENSLEY holds four university degrees in literature and linguistics, including a Ph.D. from Ball State University. He is a contributing editor and monthly columnist for *Writer's Inspirational Newsletter, National Home Business Report, ShopTalk,* and *Pace* (Piedmont Airline's in-flight magazine). He is a regional correspondent for *Writer's Digest* and a member of the editorial board of the *Ball State University Forum* literary quarterly.

Dr. Hensley is the author of numerous books, including *Writing for Profit* (Thomas Nelson Co.), *The Freelancer* (Poetica Press), *Positive Workaholism* and *Uncommon Sense* (R & R Newkirk), and *Jack London Masterplots* (Quintessence). His 1,500 freelance articles have appeared in *Downbeat, Essence, Reader's Digest, Stereo, The American Bar Association Journal, The Writer,* and *Success,* among many others.

With co-author Holly G. Miller, Dr. Hensley has written such novels as *The Legacy of Lillian Parker* and *The Caribbean Conspiracy* (Harvest House) under the pen name of Leslie Holden.

HOLLY G. MILLER is a professor of public relations at Anderson University. She holds a B.A. degree from Indiana University and an M.A. degree from Ball State University. She is a regional correspondent for *Writer's Digest* and a contributing editor to *Saturday Evening Post* and *Indianapolis* magazines. She is the recipient of more than forty writing awards from a variety of writers' associations, including The Associated Press and the National Federation of Press Women.

After serving as senior editor of *Saturday Evening Post* and as associate editor of *Country Gentleman,* Mrs. Miller worked as a public relations executive with a division of General Motors. She has co-authored two nonfiction books for Zondervan Publishing Company *First Person Singular* and *The Power Lift.* Her short stories, interviews, and features have appeared in *Young World, Today's Christian Woman, Writer's Yearbook, The Christian Writer, Reader's Digest, TV Guide,* as well as numerous newspapers and trade journals.

Among other experiences, Mrs. Miller has worked as managing editor of the *Anderson Herald* newspaper and has taught at more than two dozen writers' conferences and workshops. With Dennis E. Hensley, Mrs. Miller developed the cassette tape training series, "Writing for Prestige and Profit."